MznLnx

Missing Links Exam Preps

Exam Prep for

Marketing

Pride, Ferrell, 12th Edition

The MznLnx Exam Prep is your link from the texbook and lecture to your exams.
The MznLnx Exam Preps are unauthorized and comprehensive reviews of your textbooks.

MznLnx

Rico
Publications

Exam Prep for Marketing
12th Edition
Pride, Ferrell

Publisher: Raymond Houge
Assistant Editor: Michael Rouger
Text and Cover Designer: Lisa Buckner
Marketing Manager: Sara Swagger
Project Manager, Editorial Production: Jerry Emerson
Art Director: Vernon Lowerui

Product Manager: Dave Mason
Editorial Assitant: Rachel Guzmanji
Pedagogy: Debra Long
Cover Image: Jim Reed/Getty Images
Text and Cover Printer: City Printing, Inc.
Compositor: Media Mix, Inc.

For more information about our products, contact us at:
Dave.Mason@RicoPublications.com

For permission to use material from this text or product, submit a request online to:
Dave.Mason@RicoPublications.com

Printed in the United States
ISBN:

Contents

Contents (Cont.)

TO THE STUDENT

COMPREHENSIVE

The *MznLnx* Exam Prep series is designed to help you pass your exams. Editors at MznLnx review your textbooks and then prepare these practice exams to help you master the textbook material. Unlike study guides, workbooks, and practice tests provided by the texbook publisher and textbook authors, *MznLnx* gives you ***all*** of the material in each chapter in exam form, not just samples, so you can be sure to nail your exam.

MECHANICAL

The MznLnx Exam Prep series creates exams that will help you learn the subject matter as well as test you on your understanding. Each question is designed to help you master the concept. Just working through the exams, you gain an understanding of the subject--its a simple mechanical process that produces success.

INTEGRATED STUDY GUIDE AND REVIEW

MznLnx is not just a set of exams designed to test you, its also a comprehensive review of the subject content. Each exam question is also a review of the concept, making sure that you will get the answer correct without having to go to other sources of material. You learn as you go! Its the easiest way to pass an exam.

HUMOR

Studying can be tedious and dry. MznLnx's instructional design includes moderate humor within the exam questions on occassion, to break the tedium and revitalize the brain

1. _________ is defined by the American _________ Association as the activity, set of institutions, and processes for creating, communicating, delivering, and exchanging offerings that have value for customers, clients, partners, and society at large. The term developed from the original meaning which referred literally to going to market, as in shopping, or going to a market to sell goods or services.

_________ practice tends to be seen as a creative industry, which includes advertising, distribution and selling.

a. Product naming
b. Customer acquisition management
c. Marketing
d. Marketing myopia

2. _________ involves disseminating information about a product, product line, brand, or company. It is one of the four key aspects of the marketing mix. (The other three elements are product marketing, pricing, and distribution). P>_________ is generally sub-divided into two parts:

- Above the line _________: Promotion in the media (e.g. TV, radio, newspapers, Internet and Mobile Phones) in which the advertiser pays an advertising agency to place the ad
- Below the line _________: All other _________. Much of this is intended to be subtle enough for the consumer to be unaware that _________ is taking place. E.g. sponsorship, product placement, endorsements, sales _________, merchandising, direct mail, personal selling, public relations, trade shows

a. Cashmere Agency
b. Promotion
c. Davie Brown Index
d. Bottling lines

3. _________ is a business term meaning the market segment to which a particular good or service is marketed. It is mainly defined by age, gender, geography, socio-economic grouping, technographic, or any other combination of demographics. It is generally studied and mapped by an organization through lists and reports containing demographic information that may have an effect on the marketing of key products or services.

a. Brando
b. Category Development Index
c. Distribution
d. Market specialization

4. The Oxford University Press defines _________ as 'marketing on a worldwide scale reconciling or taking commercial advantage of global operational differences, similarities and opportunities in order to meet global objectives.' Oxford University Press' Glossary of Marketing Terms.

Here are three reasons for the shift from domestic to _________ as given by the authors of the textbook, _________ Management--3rd Edition by Masaaki Kotabe and Kristiaan Helsen, 2004.

One of the product categories in which global competition has been easy to track is in U.S. automotive sales.

a. Diversity marketing
b. Digital marketing
c. Global marketing
d. Guerrilla Marketing

5. _________ is the identity of a group or culture, or of an individual as far as one is influenced by one's belonging to a group or culture. _________ is similar to and has overlaps with, but is not synonymous with, identity politics.

There are modern questions of culture that are transferred into questions of identity.

a. 180SearchAssistant
b. Power III
c. 6-3-5 Brainwriting
d. Cultural identity

6. _________, also referred to as i-marketing, web marketing, online marketing is the marketing of products or services over the Internet.

The Internet has brought many unique benefits to marketing, one of which being lower costs for the distribution of information and media to a global audience. The interactive nature of _________, both in terms of providing instant response and eliciting responses, is a unique quality of the medium.

a. ADTECH
b. ACNielsen
c. Internet marketing
d. AMAX

7. The _________ is generally accepted as the use and specification of the four p's describing the strategic position of a product in the marketplace. One version of the origins of the _________ starts in 1948 when James Culliton said that a marketing decision should be a result of something similar to a recipe. This version continued in 1953 when Neil Borden, in his American Marketing Association presidential address, took the recipe idea one step further and coined the term 'Marketing-Mix'.

a. 6-3-5 Brainwriting
b. 180SearchAssistant
c. Power III
d. Marketing mix

8. _________s are used in open sentences. For instance, in the formula x + 1 = 5, x is a _________ which represents an 'unknown' number. _________s are often represented by letters of the Roman alphabet, or those of other alphabets, such as Greek, and use other special symbols.

a. Personalization
b. Quantitative
c. Book of business
d. Variable

9. _________ is one of the four elements of marketing mix. An organization or set of organizations (go-betweens) involved in the process of making a product or service available for use or consumption by a consumer or business user.

The other three parts of the marketing mix are product, pricing, and promotion.

a. Japan Advertising Photographers' Association
b. Comparison-Shopping agent
c. Distribution
d. Better Living Through Chemistry

10. _________ in economics and business is the result of an exchange and from that trade we assign a numerical monetary value to a good, service or asset. If I trade 4 apples for an orange, the _________ of an orange is 4 - apples. Inversely, the _________ of an apple is 1/4 oranges.

a. Pricing
b. Discounts and allowances
c. Contribution margin-based pricing
d. Price

11. The _________ is a marketing term and refers to all of the forces outside of marketing that affect marketing management's ability to build and maintain successful relationships with target customers. The _________ consists of both the macroenvironment and the microenvironment.

The microenvironment refers to the forces that are close to the company and affect its ability to serve its customers.

a. Customer franchise
b. Psychographic
c. Business-to-consumer
d. Market environment

12. _________ refers to messages and related media used to communicate with a market. Those who practice advertising, branding, direct marketing, graphic design, marketing, packaging, promotion, publicity, sponsorship, public relations, sales, sales promotion and online marketing are termed marketing communicators, _________ managers, or more briefly as marcom managers.

a. Sales promotion
b. Merchandise
c. Marketing communication
d. Merchandising

13. A _________ dominated business thought from the beginning of capitalism to the mid 1950s, and some argue it still exists in some industries. Business concerned itself primarily with production, manufacturing, and efficiency issues. Say's Law encapsulated this viewpoint, stating: 'Supply creates its own demand'.

a. Production orientation
b. Marketing
c. Blitz QFD
d. Product differentiation

14. _________ is a form of marketing developed from direct response marketing campaigns conducted in the 1970's and 1980's which emphasizes customer retention and satisfaction, rather than a dominant focus on 'point of sale' transactions.

_________ differs from other forms of marketing in that it recognizes the long term value to the firm of keeping customers, as opposed to direct or 'Intrusion' marketing, which focuses upon acquisition of new clients by targeting majority demographics based upon prospective client lists.

_________ refers to long-term and mutually beneficial arrangement wherein both buyer and seller focus on value enhancement through the certain of more satisfying exchange.This approach attempts to transcend the simple purchase exchange process with customer to make more meaningful and richer contact by providing a more holistic, personalized purchase, and use orn consumption experience to create stronger ties.

a. Relationship marketing
b. Global marketing
c. Diversity marketing
d. Guerrilla Marketing

15. _________ consists of the processes a company uses to track and organize its contacts with its current and prospective customers. _________ software is used to support these processes; information about customers and customer interactions can be entered, stored and accessed by employees in different company departments. Typical _________ goals are to improve services provided to customers, and to use customer contact information for targeted marketing.

a. Demand generation
b. Product bundling
c. Commercialization
d. Customer relationship management

16. Customer _________ consists of the processes a company uses to track and organize its contacts with its current and prospective customers. CRelationship management software is used to support these processes; information about customers and customer interactions can be entered, stored and accessed by employees in different company departments. Typical CRelationship management goals are to improve services provided to customers, and to use customer contact information for targeted marketing.

a. Product bundling
b. Marketing
c. Green marketing
d. Relationship management

17. A personal and cultural _________ is a relative ethic _________, an assumption upon which implementation can be extrapolated. A _________ system is a set of consistent _________s and measures that is soo not true. A principle _________ is a foundation upon which other _________s and measures of integrity are based.

a. Perceptual maps
b. Package-on-Package
c. Value
d. Supreme Court of the United States

18. _________ is a business discipline which is focused on the practical application of marketing techniques and the management of a firm's marketing resources and activities. Marketing managers are often responsible for influencing the level, timing, and composition of customer demand accepted definition of the term. In part, this is because the role of a marketing manager can vary significantly based on a business' size, corporate culture, and industry context.

a. Marketing management
b. Door-to-door
c. Business structure
d. Performance-based advertising

1. _________ is an organization's process of defining its strategy and making decisions on allocating its resources to pursue this strategy, including its capital and people. Various business analysis techniques can be used in _________, including SWOT analysis (Strengths, Weaknesses, Opportunities, and Threats) and PEST analysis (Political, Economic, Social, and Technological analysis) or STEER analysis involving Socio-cultural, Technological, Economic, Ecological, and Regulatory factors and EPISTEL (Environment, Political, Informatic, Social, Technological, Economic and Legal)

_________ is the formal consideration of an organization's future course. All _________ deals with at least one of three key questions:

1. 'What do we do?'
2. 'For whom do we do it?'
3. 'How do we excel?'

In business _________, the third question is better phrased 'How can we beat or avoid competition?'. (Bradford and Duncan, page 1.)

a. Power III
b. 180SearchAssistant
c. 6-3-5 Brainwriting
d. Strategic planning

2. _________ in organizations and public policy is both the organizational process of creating and maintaining a plan; and the psychological process of thinking about the activities required to create a desired goal on some scale. As such, it is a fundamental property of intelligent behavior. This thought process is essential to the creation and refinement of a plan, or integration of it with other plans, that is, it combines forecasting of developments with the preparation of scenarios of how to react to them.

a. Planning
b. Power III
c. 6-3-5 Brainwriting
d. 180SearchAssistant

3. _________ is defined by the American _________ Association as the activity, set of institutions, and processes for creating, communicating, delivering, and exchanging offerings that have value for customers, clients, partners, and society at large. The term developed from the original meaning which referred literally to going to market, as in shopping, or going to a market to sell goods or services.

_________ practice tends to be seen as a creative industry, which includes advertising, distribution and selling.

a. Product naming
b. Marketing myopia
c. Customer acquisition management
d. Marketing

4. The _________ is a marketing term and refers to all of the forces outside of marketing that affect marketing management's ability to build and maintain successful relationships with target customers. The _________ consists of both the macroenvironment and the microenvironment.

The microenvironment refers to the forces that are close to the company and affect its ability to serve its customers.

a. Customer franchise
b. Business-to-consumer
c. Psychographic
d. Market environment

5. A _________ is a written document that details the necessary actions to achieve one or more marketing objectives. It can be for a product or service, a brand, or a product line. _________s cover between one and five years.

a. Prosumer
b. Marketing strategy
c. Disruptive technology
d. Marketing plan

6. A _________ is a process that can allow an organization to concentrate its limited resources on the greatest opportunities to increase sales and achieve a sustainable competitive advantage. A _________ should be centered around the key concept that customer satisfaction is the main goal.

A _________ is most effective when it is an integral component of corporate strategy, defining how the organization will successfully engage customers, prospects, and competitors in the market arena.

a. Cyberdoc
b. Societal marketing
c. Psychographic
d. Marketing strategy

7. Human beings are also considered to be _________ because they have the ability to change raw materials into valuable _________. The term Human _________ can also be defined as the skills, energies, talents, abilities and knowledge that are used for the production of goods or the rendering of services. While taking into account human beings as _________, the following things have to be kept in mind:

- The size of the population
- The capabilities of the individuals in that population

Many _________ cannot be consumed in their original form. They have to be processed in order to change them into more usable commodities.

a. 180SearchAssistant
b. Power III
c. 6-3-5 Brainwriting
d. Resources

8. _________ can be regarded as an outcome of mental processes (cognitive process) leading to the selection of a course of action among several alternatives. Every _________ process produces a final choice. The output can be an action or an opinion of choice.

a. Power III
b. 180SearchAssistant
c. 6-3-5 Brainwriting
d. Decision making

9. Competitiveness is a comparative concept of the ability and performance of a firm, sub-sector or country to sell and supply goods and/or services in a given market. Although widely used in economics and business management, the usefulness of the concept, particularly in the context of national competitiveness, is vigorously disputed by economists, such as Paul Krugman .

The term may also be applied to markets, where it is used to refer to the extent to which the market structure may be regarded as perfectly _________.

a. Free trade zone
b. Geographical pricing
c. Competitive
d. Customs union

10. _________ is, in very basic words, a position a firm occupies against its competitors.

According to Michael Porter, the three methods for creating a sustainable _________ are through:

1. Cost leadership - Cost advantage occurs when a firm delivers the same services as its competitors but at a lower cost;

2.

a. Competitive advantage
b. 180SearchAssistant
c. Power III
d. 6-3-5 Brainwriting

11. Core competency is something that a firm can do well and that meets the following three conditions:

1. It provides consumer benefits
2. It is not easy for competitors to imitate
3. It can be leveraged widely to many products and markets.

A core competency can take various forms, including technical/subject matter know how, a reliable process, and/or close relationships with customers and suppliers (Mascarenhas et al. 1998.) It may also include product development or culture, such as employee dedication.

_________ are particular strengths relative to other organizations in the industry which provide the fundamental basis for the provision of added value.

a. Power III
b. Core competencies
c. 6-3-5 Brainwriting
d. 180SearchAssistant

12. A _________ is a brief statement of the purpose of a company, organization. It is ideally used to guide the actions of the organization.

_________s often contain the following:

- Purpose of the organization
- The organization's primary stakeholders: clients, stockholders, etc.
- Responsibilities of the organization towards these stockholders
- Products and services offered

Generally shorter _________s are more effective than longer ones.

In developing a _________:

- Encourage input as feasible from employees, volunteers, and other stakeholders
- Publicize it broadly

The _________ can be used to resolve differences between business stakeholders. Stakeholders include: employees including managers and executives, stockholders, board of directors, customers, suppliers, distributors, creditors, governments (local, state, federal, etc.), unions, competitors, NGO's, and the general public.

a. Power III
b. 6-3-5 Brainwriting
c. 180SearchAssistant
d. Mission statement

13. Organizational culture is not the same as _________. It is wider and deeper concepts, something that an organization 'is' rather than what it 'has' (according to Buchanan and Huczynski.)

_________ is the total sum of the values, customs, traditions and meanings that make a company unique.

a. Cross-functional team
b. Corporate culture
c. 180SearchAssistant
d. Power III

14. _________ refers to the overarching strategy of the diversified firm. Such a _________ answers the questions of 'in which businesses should we be in?' and 'how does being in these business create synergy and/or add to the competitive advantage of the corporation as a whole?'

Business strategy refers to the aggregated strategies of single business firm or a strategic business unit (SBU) in a diversified corporation. According to Michael Porter, a firm must formulate a business strategy that incorporates either cost leadership, differentiation or focus in order to achieve a sustainable competitive advantage and long-term success in its chosen arenas or industries.

a. Strategic business unit
b. Business strategy
c. Strategic group
d. Corporate strategy

15. _________ is difficult to define. For example, in 1952, Alfred Kroeber and Clyde Kluckhohn compiled a list of 164 definitions of '_________' in _________: A Critical Review of Concepts and Definitions. However, the word '_________' is most commonly used in three basic senses:

- excellence of taste in the fine arts and humanities
- an integrated pattern of human knowledge, belief, and behavior that depends upon the capacity for symbolic thought and social learning
- the set of shared attitudes, values, goals, and practices that characterizes an institution, organization or group.

When the concept first emerged in eighteenth- and nineteenth-century Europe, it connoted a process of cultivation or improvement, as in agriculture or horticulture. In the nineteenth century, it came to refer first to the betterment or refinement of the individual, especially through education, and then to the fulfillment of national aspirations or ideals.

a. African Americans
b. AStore
c. Albert Einstein
d. Culture

16. A _________ is a plan of action designed to achieve a particular goal.

_________ is different from tactics. In military terms, tactics is concerned with the conduct of an engagement while _________ is concerned with how different engagements are linked.

a. Power III
b. Strategy
c. 6-3-5 Brainwriting
d. 180SearchAssistant

17. In business, a _________ is a product or a business unit that generates unusually high profit margins: so high that it is responsible for a large amount of a company's operating profit. This profit far exceeds the amount necessary to maintain the _________ business, and the excess is used by the business for other purposes.

A firm is said to be acting as a _________ when its earnings per share (EPS) is equal to its dividends per share (DPS), or in other words, when a firm pays out 100% of its free cash flow (FCF) to its shareholders as dividends at the end of each accounting term.

a. Cash cow
b. Goal setting
c. Crisis management
d. Corporate transparency

18. _________, in strategic management and marketing, is the percentage or proportion of the total available market or market segment that is being serviced by a company. It can be expressed as a company's sales revenue (from that market) divided by the total sales revenue available in that market. It can also be expressed as a company's unit sales volume (in a market) divided by the total volume of units sold in that market.

a. Customer relationship management
b. Demand generation
c. Cyberdoc
d. Market share

19. _________ is understood as a business unit within the overall corporate identity which is distinguishable from other business because it serves a defined external market where management can conduct strategic planning in relation to products and markets. When companies become really large, they are best thought of as being composed of a number of businesses (or _________s.)

In the broader domain of strategic management, the phrase '_________' came into use in the 1960s, largely as a result of General Electric's many units.

a. Business strategy
b. Corporate strategy
c. Strategic business unit
d. Cost leadership

20. _________ is a business term meaning the market segment to which a particular good or service is marketed. It is mainly defined by age, gender, geography, socio-economic grouping, technographic, or any other combination of demographics. It is generally studied and mapped by an organization through lists and reports containing demographic information that may have an effect on the marketing of key products or services.

a. Distribution
b. Market specialization
c. Category Development Index
d. Brando

21. _________ in economics and business is the result of an exchange and from that trade we assign a numerical monetary value to a good, service or asset. If I trade 4 apples for an orange, the _________ of an orange is 4 - apples. Inversely, the _________ of an apple is 1/4 oranges.

a. Pricing
b. Discounts and allowances
c. Contribution margin-based pricing
d. Price

22. The _________ is generally accepted as the use and specification of the four p's describing the strategic position of a product in the marketplace. One version of the origins of the _________ starts in 1948 when James Culliton said that a marketing decision should be a result of something similar to a recipe. This version continued in 1953 when Neil Borden, in his American Marketing Association presidential address, took the recipe idea one step further and coined the term 'Marketing-Mix'.

a. 180SearchAssistant
b. 6-3-5 Brainwriting
c. Power III
d. Marketing mix

23. _________ is a term used in business for a short document that summarises a longer report, proposal or group of related reports in such a way that readers can rapidly become acquainted with a large body of material without having to read it all. It will usually contain a brief statement of the problem or proposal covered in the major document(s), background information, concise analysis and main conclusions. It is intended as an aid to decision making by business managers.

a. ADTECH
b. AMAX
c. ACNielsen
d. Executive summary

24. _________ is a strategic planning method used to evaluate the Strengths, Weaknesses, Opportunities, and Threats involved in a project or in a business venture. It involves specifying the objective of the business venture or project and identifying the internal and external factors that are favorable and unfavorable to achieving that objective. The technique is credited to Albert Humphrey, who led a research project at Stanford University in the 1960s and 1970s using data from Fortune 500 companies.

a. Market environment
b. SWOT analysis
c. Lead scoring
d. Product differentiation

25. _________ is one of the four elements of marketing mix. An organization or set of organizations (go-betweens) involved in the process of making a product or service available for use or consumption by a consumer or business user.

The other three parts of the marketing mix are product, pricing, and promotion.

a. Japan Advertising Photographers' Association
b. Better Living Through Chemistry
c. Distribution
d. Comparison-Shopping agent

26. _________ involves disseminating information about a product, product line, brand, or company. It is one of the four key aspects of the marketing mix. (The other three elements are product marketing, pricing, and distribution). P>_________ is generally sub-divided into two parts:

- Above the line _________: Promotion in the media (e.g. TV, radio, newspapers, Internet and Mobile Phones) in which the advertiser pays an advertising agency to place the ad
- Below the line _________: All other _________. Much of this is intended to be subtle enough for the consumer to be unaware that _________ is taking place. E.g. sponsorship, product placement, endorsements, sales _________, merchandising, direct mail, personal selling, public relations, trade shows

a. Cashmere Agency
b. Bottling lines
c. Davie Brown Index
d. Promotion

27.

Competitive advantage is, in very basic words, a position a firm occupies against its competitors. According to Michael Porter, the three methods for creating a _________ are through:

Cost leadership - Cost advantage occurs when a firm delivers the same services as its competitors but at a lower cost;

Differentiation - Differentiation advantage occurs when a firm delivers greater services for the same price of its competitors. They are collectively known as positional advantages because they denote the firm's position in its industry as a leader in either superior services or cost;

Focus (economics) - A focused approach requires the firm to concentrate on a narrow, exclusive competitive segment (market niche), hoping to achieve a local rather than industry wide competitive advantage. There are cost focus seekers, who aim to obtain a local cost advantage over competition and differentiation focuser, who are looking for a local difference.

a. Sustainable competitive advantage
b. 180SearchAssistant
c. 6-3-5 Brainwriting
d. Power III

28. _________ is the realization of an application idea, model, design, specification, standard, algorithm an _________ is a realization of a technical specification or algorithm as a program, software component, or other computer system. Many _________s may exist for a given specification or standard.

a. AMAX
b. Implementation
c. ADTECH
d. ACNielsen

29. _________ is systematic determination of merit, worth, and significance of something or someone using criteria against a set of standards. _________ often is used to characterize and appraise subjects of interest in a wide range of human enterprises, including the arts, criminal justice, foundations and non-profit organizations, government, health care, and other human services.

Depending on the topic of interest, there are professional groups which look to the quality and rigor of the _________ process.

a. ACNielsen
b. Evaluation
c. AMAX
d. ADTECH

30. _________ is a form of communication that typically attempts to persuade potential customers to purchase or to consume more of a particular brand of product or service. 'While now central to the contemporary global economy and the reproduction of global production networks, it is only quite recently that _________ has been more than a marginal influence on patterns of sales and production. The formation of modern _________ was intimately bound up with the emergence of new forms of monopoly capitalism around the end of the 19th and beginning of the 20th century as one element in corporate strategies to create, organize and where possible control markets, especially for mass produced consumer goods.

a. AMAX
b. Advertising
c. ADTECH
d. ACNielsen

1. _________ is defined by the American _________ Association as the activity, set of institutions, and processes for creating, communicating, delivering, and exchanging offerings that have value for customers, clients, partners, and society at large. The term developed from the original meaning which referred literally to going to market, as in shopping, or going to a market to sell goods or services.

_________ practice tends to be seen as a creative industry, which includes advertising, distribution and selling.

a. Marketing myopia
b. Product naming
c. Customer acquisition management
d. Marketing

2. The _________ is a marketing term and refers to all of the forces outside of marketing that affect marketing management's ability to build and maintain successful relationships with target customers. The _________ consists of both the macroenvironment and the microenvironment.

The microenvironment refers to the forces that are close to the company and affect its ability to serve its customers.

a. Market environment
b. Customer franchise
c. Psychographic
d. Business-to-consumer

3. _________ is a process of gathering, analyzing, and dispensing information for tactical or strategic purposes. The _________ process entails obtaining both factual and subjective information on the business environments in which a company is operating or considering entering.

There are three ways of scanning the business environment:

- Ad-hoc scanning - Short term, infrequent examinations usually initiated by a crisis
- Regular scanning - Studies done on a regular schedule (say, once a year)
- Continuous scanning(also called continuous learning) - continuous structured data collection and processing on a broad range of environmental factors

Most commentators feel that in today's turbulent business environment the best scanning method available is continuous scanning.This allows the firm to :

-act quickly-take advantage of opportunities before competitors do-respond to environmental threats before significant damage is done

The Macro Environment

_________ usually refers just to the macro environment, but it can also include:-industry -competitor analysis -marketing research(consumer analysis) -New Product Development(product innovations)- the company's internal environment

Macro _________ involves analysing:

- The Economy

GDP per capitaeconomic growthunemployment]] rateinflation]] rateconsumer and investor confidenceinventory levelscurrency exchange ratesmerchandise trade balancefinancial and political health of trading partnersbalance of paymentsfuture trends

- Government

political climate - amount of government activitypolitical stability and riskgovernment debtbudget deficit or surpluscorporate and personal tax ratespayroll taxesimport tariffs and quotasexport restrictionsrestrictions on international financial flows

- Legal

minimum wage lawsenvironmental protection lawsworker safety lawsunion lawscopyright and patent lawsanti- monopoly lawsSunday closing lawsmunicipal licenceslaws that favour business investment

- Technology

efficiency of infrastructure, including: roads, ports, airports, rolling stock, hospitals, education, healthcare, communication, etc.industrial productivitynew manufacturing processesnew products and services of competitorsnew products and services of supply chain partnersany new technology that could impact the companycost and accessibility of electrical power

- Ecology
  - ecological concerns that affect the firms production processes
  - ecological concerns that affect customers' buying habits
  - ecological concerns that affect customers' perception of the company or product
- Socio-Cultural
  - demographic factors such as:
    - population size and distribution
    - age distribution
    - education levels
    - income levels
    - ethnic origins
    - religious affiliations
  - attitudes towards:
    - materialism, capitalism, free enterprise
    - individualism, role of family, role of government, collectivism
    - role of church and religion
    - consumerism
    - environmentalism
    - importance of work, pride of accomplishment
  - cultural structures including:
    - diet and nutrition
    - housing conditions
- Potential Suppliers
  - Labour supply
    - quantity of labour available
    - quality of labour available
    - stability of labour supply
    - wage expectations
    - employee turn-over rate
    - strikes and labour relations
    - educational facilities
  - Material suppliers
    - quality, quantity, price, and stability of material inputs
    - delivery delays
    - proximity of bulky or heavy material inputs
    - level of competition among suppliers
  - Service Providers
    - quantity, quality, price, and stability of service facilitators
    - special requirements
- Stakeholders
  - Lobbyists
  - Shareholders
  - Employees
  - Partners

Scanning these macro environmental variables for threats and opportunities requires that each issue be rated on two dimensions. It must be rated on its potential impact on the company, and rated on its likeliness of occurrence.

a. ACNielsen
b. Environmental scanning
c. AMAX
d. ADTECH

4. Competitiveness is a comparative concept of the ability and performance of a firm, sub-sector or country to sell and supply goods and/or services in a given market. Although widely used in economics and business management, the usefulness of the concept, particularly in the context of national competitiveness, is vigorously disputed by economists, such as Paul Krugman .

The term may also be applied to markets, where it is used to refer to the extent to which the market structure may be regarded as perfectly _________.

a. Competitive
b. Customs union
c. Geographical pricing
d. Free trade zone

5. The Oxford University Press defines _________ as 'marketing on a worldwide scale reconciling or taking commercial advantage of global operational differences, similarities and opportunities in order to meet global objectives.' Oxford University Press' Glossary of Marketing Terms.

Here are three reasons for the shift from domestic to _________ as given by the authors of the textbook, _________ Management--3rd Edition by Masaaki Kotabe and Kristiaan Helsen, 2004.

One of the product categories in which global competition has been easy to track is in U.S. automotive sales.

a. Digital marketing
b. Global marketing
c. Guerrilla Marketing
d. Diversity marketing

6. _________, also referred to as i-marketing, web marketing, online marketing is the marketing of products or services over the Internet.

The Internet has brought many unique benefits to marketing, one of which being lower costs for the distribution of information and media to a global audience. The interactive nature of _________, both in terms of providing instant response and eliciting responses, is a unique quality of the medium.

a. ACNielsen
b. ADTECH
c. AMAX
d. Internet marketing

7. Regulation refers to 'controlling human or societal behaviour by rules or restrictions.' Regulation can take many forms: legal restrictions promulgated by a government authority, self-regulation, social regulation (e.g. norms), co-regulation and market regulation. One can consider regulation as actions of conduct imposing sanctions (such as a fine.) This action of administrative law, or implementing _________ law, may be contrasted with statutory or case law.

a. Regulatory
b. Robinson-Patman Act
c. Privacy law
d. Right to Financial Privacy Act

8. _________ is a rivalry between individuals, groups, nations for territory, a niche, or allocation of resources. It arises whenever two or more parties strive for a goal which cannot be shared. _________ occurs naturally between living organisms which co-exist in the same environment.

a. Price competition
b. Competition
c. Non-price competition
d. Price fixing

9. A _________ is a collection of symbols, experiences and associations connected with a product, a service, a person or any other artifact or entity.

_________s have become increasingly important components of culture and the economy, now being described as 'cultural accessories and personal philosophies'.

Some people distinguish the psychological aspect of a _________ from the experiential aspect.

a. Brand equity
b. Brandable software
c. Store brand
d. Brand

10. _________ is a common market form. Many markets can be considered monopolistically competitive, often including the markets for restaurants, cereal, clothing, shoes and service industries in large cities. Short-run equilibrium of the firm under

____

Monopolistically competitive markets have the following characteristics:

- There are many producers and many consumers in a given market, and no business has total control over the market price.
- Consumers perceive that there are non-price differences among the competitors' products.
- There are few barriers to entry and exit.
- Producers have a degree of control over price.

Long-run equilibrium of the firm under _________

The characteristics of a monopolistically competitive market are almost the same as in perfect competition, with the exception of heterogeneous products, and that _________ involves a great deal of non-price competition (based on subtle product differentiation.) A firm making profits in the short run will break even in the long run because demand will decrease and average total cost will increase.

a. Macroeconomics
b. Gross domestic product
c. Monopolistic competition
d. Recession

11. In economics, a _________ exists when a specific individual or enterprise has sufficient control over a particular product or service to determine significantly the terms on which other individuals shall have access to it. Monopolies are thus characterized by a lack of economic competition for the good or service that they provide and a lack of viable substitute goods. The verb 'monopolize' refers to the process by which a firm gains persistently greater market share than what is expected under perfect competition.

a. Power III
b. 6-3-5 Brainwriting
c. Monopoly
d. 180SearchAssistant

12. _________ generally refers to a list of all planned expenses and revenues. It is a plan for saving and spending. A _________ is an important concept in microeconomics, which uses a _________ line to illustrate the trade-offs between two or more goods.

a. Budget
b. Power III
c. 6-3-5 Brainwriting
d. 180SearchAssistant

13. An _________ is a market form in which a market or industry is dominated by a small number of sellers (oligopolists.) Because there are few participants in this type of market, each oligopolist is aware of the actions of the others. The decisions of one firm influence, and are influenced by, the decisions of other firms.

a. ACNielsen
b. AMAX
c. Oligopoly
d. ADTECH

14. The term _________ refers to economy-wide fluctuations in production or economic activity over several months or years. These fluctuations occur around a long-term growth trend, and typically involve shifts over time between periods of relatively rapid economic growth (expansion or boom), and periods of relative stagnation or decline (contraction or recession.)

These fluctuations are often measured using the growth rate of real gross domestic product.

a. Market structure
b. Monopolistic competition
c. Business cycle
d. Perfect competition

15. In economics, the term _________ describes the reduction of a country's gross domestic product (GDP) for at least two quarters. The usual dictionary definition is 'a period of reduced economic activity', a business cycle contraction.

The United States-based National Bureau of Economic Research (NBER) defines economic _________ as: 'a significant decline in [the] economic activity spread across the country, lasting more than a few months, normally visible in real GDP growth, real personal income, employment (non-farm payrolls), industrial production, and wholesale-retail sales.' The NBER's Business Cycle Dating Committee is generally seen as the authority for dating US _________s.

a. Recession
b. Law of demand
c. Leading indicator
d. Macroeconomics

16. _________s is the social science that studies the production, distribution, and consumption of goods and services. The term _________s comes from the Ancient Greek oá¼°κονομΐα from oá¼¶κος (oikos, 'house') + νÏŒμος (nomos, 'custom' or 'law'), hence 'rules of the house(hold)'. Current _________ models developed out of the broader field of political economy in the late 19th century, owing to a desire to use an empirical approach more akin to the physical sciences.

a. ADTECH
b. ACNielsen
c. Industrial organization
d. Economic

17. _________ is income after subtracting taxes and normal expenses (such as rent or mortgage and food) to maintain a certain standard of living. It is the amount of an individual's income available for spending after the essentials (such as food, clothing, and shelter) have been taken care of:

_________ = Gross income - taxes - necessities

Despite the formal definitions above, disposable income is commonly used to denote _________. The meaning should therefore be interpreted from context.

a. Discretionary income
b. Power III
c. 6-3-5 Brainwriting
d. 180SearchAssistant

18. _________ is gross income minus income tax on that income.

Discretionary income is income after subtracting taxes and normal expenses (such as rent or mortgage and food) to maintain a certain standard of living. It is the amount of an individual's income available for spending after the essentials (such as food, clothing, and shelter) have been taken care of:

Discretionary income = Gross income - taxes - necessities

Despite the formal definitions above, _________ is commonly used to denote Discretionary income.

a. 180SearchAssistant
b. Power III
c. 6-3-5 Brainwriting
d. Disposable income

19. _________ is the practice of influencing decisions made by government. It includes all attempts to influence legislators and officials, whether by other legislators, constituents or organized groups. A lobbyist is a person who tries to influence legislation on behalf of a special interest or a member of a lobby.

a. African Americans
b. Lobbying
c. AStore
d. Albert Einstein

20. In the United States , a _________ is the name commonly given to a private group, regardless of size, organized to elect political candidates. Legally, what constitutes a '_________' for purposes of regulation is a matter of state and federal law. Under the Federal Election Campaign Act, an organization becomes a 'political committee' by receiving contributions or making expenditures in excess of $1,000 for the purpose of influencing a federal election.

a. Power III
b. 180SearchAssistant
c. 6-3-5 Brainwriting
d. Political Action Committee

21. The Celler-Derek Browne Act is a United States federal law passed in 1950 that reformed and strengthened the Clayton Antitrust Act of 1914 which had amended the Sherman Antitrust Act of 1890. The _________ was passed to close a loophole regarding certain asset acquisitions and acquisitions involving firms that were not direct competitors. While the Clayton Act prohibited stock purchase mergers that resulted in reduced competition, shrewd businessmen were able to find ways around the Clayton Act by simply buying up a competitor's assets.

a. Wheeler-Lea Act
b. Patent
c. Mediation
d. Celler-Kefauver Act

22. _________ is a broad label that refers to any individuals or households that use goods and services generated within the economy. The concept of a _________ is used in different contexts, so that the usage and significance of the term may vary.

A _________ is a person who uses any product or service.

a. 6-3-5 Brainwriting
b. Power III
c. Consumer
d. 180SearchAssistant

23. _________ are final goods specifically intended for the mass market. For instance, _________ do not include investment assets, like precious antiques, even though these antiques are final goods.

Manufactured goods are goods that have been processed by way of machinery.

a. Consumer Goods
b. Durable good
c. Power III
d. Free good

24. _________ is a form of government regulation which protects the interests of consumers. For example, a government may require businesses to disclose detailed information about products--particularly in areas where safety or public health is an issue, such as food. _________ is linked to the idea of consumer rights (that consumers have various rights as consumers), and to the formation of consumer organizations which help consumers make better choices in the marketplace.

a. Federal Bureau of Investigation
b. Sound trademark
c. Trademark dilution
d. Consumer Protection

25. _________ (or citizen-to-citizen) electronic commerce involves the electronically-facilitated transactions between consumers through some third party. A common example is the online auction, in which a consumer posts an item for sale and other consumers bid to purchase it; the third party generally charges a flat fee or commission. The sites are only intermediaries, just there to match consumers.

a. Web banner
b. Locator software
c. Business-to-government
d. Consumer-to-consumer

26. _________ is a form of intellectual property which gives the creator of an original work exclusive rights for a certain time period in relation to that work, including its publication, distribution and adaptation; after which time the work is said to enter the public domain. _________ applies to any expressible form of an idea or information that is substantive and discrete. Some jurisdictions also recognize 'moral rights' of the creator of a work, such as the right to be credited for the work.

a. Celler-Kefauver Act
b. Reasonable person standard
c. Collective mark
d. Copyright

27. A _________ product is an imitation which infringes upon a production monopoly held by either a state or corporation. Goods are produced with the intent to bypass this monopoly and thus take advantage of the established worth of the previous product. The word _________ frequently describes both the forgeries of currency and documents, as well as the imitations of clothing, software, pharmaceuticals, watches, electronics, and company logos and brands.

a. Counterfeit
b. 180SearchAssistant
c. Power III
d. 6-3-5 Brainwriting

28. The _________ is a United States copyright law that implements two 1996 treaties of the World Intellectual Property Organization (WIPO.) It criminalizes production and dissemination of technology, devices whether or not there is actual infringement of copyright itself. In addition, the _________ heightens the penalties for copyright infringement on the Internet.

a. Copyright infringement
b. Priority right
c. Regulatory
d. Digital Millennium Copyright Act

29. The _________ is a US law that applies to labels on many consumer products. It requires the label to state:

- The identity of the product;
- The name and place of business of the manufacturer, packer, or distributor; and
- The net quantity of contents.

The contents statement must include both metric and U.S. customary units.

Passed under Lyndon B. Johnson in 1966, the law first took effect on July 1, 1967. The metric labeling requirement was added in 1992 and took effect on February 14, 1994.

a. 6-3-5 Brainwriting
b. 180SearchAssistant
c. Power III
d. Fair Packaging and Labeling Act

30. The _________ is an independent agency of the United States government, established in 1914 by the _________ Act. Its principal mission is the promotion of 'consumer protection' and the elimination and prevention of what regulators perceive to be harmfully 'anti-competitive' business practices, such as coercive monopoly.

The _________ Act was one of President Wilson's major acts against trusts.

a. 6-3-5 Brainwriting
b. Federal Trade Commission
c. Power III
d. 180SearchAssistant

31. The _________ of 1914 (15 U.S.C Â§Â§ 41-58, as amended) established the Federal Trade Commission (FTC), a bipartisan body of five members appointed by the President of the United States for seven year terms. This Commission was authorized to issue Cease and Desist orders to large corporations to curb unfair trade practices. This Act also gave more flexibility to the US congress for judicial matters.

a. Product liability
b. Comparative negligence
c. Federal Trade Commission Act
d. Gripe site

32. The _________ is a United States federal law (15 U.S.C. Â§ 2301 et seq.). Enacted in 1975, it is the federal statute that governs warranties on consumer products.

The statute is remedial in nature and is intended to protect consumers from deceptive warranty practices. Consumer products are not required to have warranties, but if one is given, it must comply with the _________.

a. Confusing similarity
b. Singapore Treaty on the Law of Trademarks
c. Community Trade Mark
d. Magnuson-Moss Warranty Act

33. The _________ is a 1990 United States Federal law. It was signed into law on November 8, 1990 by the president.

The law gives the Food and Drug Administration (FDA) authority to require nutrition labeling of most foods regulated by the Agency; and to require that all nutrient content claims (for example, 'high fiber', 'low fat', etc).

a. Copyright infringement
b. Trespass to land
c. Fair Debt Collection Practices Act
d. Nutrition Labeling and Education Act

34. _________ is one of the four Ps of the marketing mix. The other three aspects are product, promotion, and place. It is also a key variable in microeconomic price allocation theory.

a. Competitor indexing
b. Relationship based pricing
c. Price
d. Pricing

35. _________ is the ability of an individual or group to seclude themselves or information about themselves and thereby reveal themselves selectively. The boundaries and content of what is considered private differ among cultures and individuals, but share basic common themes. _________ is sometimes related to anonymity, the wish to remain unnoticed or unidentified in the public realm.

a. 6-3-5 Brainwriting
b. 180SearchAssistant
c. Power III
d. Privacy

36. The _________ of 1936 (or Anti-Price Discrimination Act, 15 U.S.C. Â§ 13) is a United States federal law that prohibits what were considered, at the time of passage, to be anticompetitive practices by producers, specifically price discrimination. It grew out of practices in which chain stores were allowed to purchase goods at lower prices than other retailers.

a. Registered trademark symbol
b. Trademark infringement
c. Fair Debt Collection Practices Act
d. Robinson-Patman Act

37. The _________ requires the Federal government to investigate and pursue trusts, companies and organizations suspected of violating the Act. It was the first United States Federal statute to limit cartels and monopolies, and today still forms the basis for most antitrust litigation by the federal government.

a. Power III
b. 180SearchAssistant
c. 6-3-5 Brainwriting
d. Sherman Antitrust Act

38. A _________ or trade mark, identified by the symbols â„¢ (not yet registered) and Â® (registered) business organization or other legal entity to identify that the products and/or services to consumers with which the _________ appears originate from a unique source of origin, and to distinguish its products or services from those of other entities. A _________ is a type of intellectual property, and typically a name, word, phrase, logo, symbol, design, image, or a combination of these elements. There is also a range of non-conventional _________s comprising marks which do not fall into these standard categories.

a. Trademark
b. Power III
c. Risk management
d. 180SearchAssistant

39. _________ is a trademark law concept permitting the owner of a famous trademark to forbid others from using that mark in a way that would lessen its uniqueness. In most cases, _________ involves an unauthorized use of another's trademark on products that do not compete with, and have little connection with, those of the trademark owner. For example, a famous trademark used by one company to refer to hair care products might be diluted if another company began using a similar mark to refer to breakfast cereals or spark plugs.

a. Trademark attorney
b. Federal Bureau of Investigation
c. Trespass to land
d. Trademark Dilution

40. Once trademark rights are established in a particular jurisdiction, these rights are generally only enforceable in that jurisdiction, a quality which is sometimes known as territoriality. However, there is a range of international _________ and systems which facilitate the protection of trademarks in more than one jurisdiction

To avoid conflicts with earlier trademark rights, it is highly recommended to conduct trademark searches before the trademarks office (or 'trademarks registry') of a particular jurisdiction--e.g. US Patent and Trademark Office.

a. Supreme Court of the United States
b. Self branding
c. Sigg bottles
d. Trademark laws

41. The _________ of 1938 is a United States federal law that amended the Federal Trade Commission Act to add the clause 'unfair or deceptive acts or practices in commerce are hereby declared unlawful' to the Section 5 prohibition of unfair methods of competition, in order to protect consumers as well as competition.

1938 amendment to the federal trade commission act that authorized the FTC to restrict unfair or deceptive acts; also called the advertising act. Until this amendment was passed, the FTC could only restrict practices that were unfair to competitors.

a. Nutrition Labeling and Education Act
b. Patent
c. Sarbanes-Oxley Act of 2002
d. Wheeler-Lea Act

42. _________ is one of the four elements of marketing mix. An organization or set of organizations (go-betweens) involved in the process of making a product or service available for use or consumption by a consumer or business user.

The other three parts of the marketing mix are product, pricing, and promotion.

a. Better Living Through Chemistry
b. Japan Advertising Photographers' Association
c. Distribution
d. Comparison-Shopping agent

43. _________ refers to 'controlling human or societal behaviour by rules or restrictions.' _________ can take many forms: legal restrictions promulgated by a government authority, self-_________, social _________, co-_________ and market _________. One can consider _________ as actions of conduct imposing sanctions (such as a fine.) This action of administrative law, or implementing regulatory law, may be contrasted with statutory or case law.

a. Non-conventional trademark
b. Rule of four
c. Regulation
d. CAN-SPAM

44. A _________ is a relatively new executive level position at a corporation, company, organization typically reporting directly to the CEO or board of directors. The _________ is responsible for a brand's image, experience, and promise, and propagating it throughout all aspects of the company. The brand officer oversees marketing, advertising, design, public relations and customer service departments.

a. Financial analyst
b. Power III
c. Chief executive officer
d. Chief brand officer

45. The United States _________ is an independent agency of the United States government created in 1972 through the Consumer Product Safety Act to protect 'against unreasonable risks of injuries associated with consumer products.' As of 2006 its acting chairman is Nancy Nord, a Republican. The other commissioner is Thomas Hill Moore, a Democrat. Normally the board has three commissioners.

a. Power III
b. 180SearchAssistant
c. 6-3-5 Brainwriting
d. Consumer Product Safety Commission

46. The _________ is an independent agency of the United States government, created, directed, and empowered by Congressional statute , and with the majority of its commissioners appointed by the current President.

a. 6-3-5 Brainwriting
b. Federal Communications Commission
c. Power III
d. 180SearchAssistant

47. The U.S. _________ is an agency of the United States Department of Health and Human Services and is responsible for regulating and supervising the safety of foods, dietary supplements, drugs, vaccines, biological medical products, blood products, medical devices, radiation-emitting devices, veterinary products, and cosmetics. The FDA also enforces section 361 of the Public Health Service Act and the associated regulations, including sanitation requirements on interstate travel as well as specific rules for control of disease on products ranging from pet turtles to semen donations for assisted reproductive medicine techniques.

The FDA is an agency within the United States Department of Health and Human Services responsible for protecting and promoting the nation's public health.

a. Power III
b. 6-3-5 Brainwriting
c. Food and Drug Administration
d. 180SearchAssistant

48. _________ is a form of communication that typically attempts to persuade potential customers to purchase or to consume more of a particular brand of product or service. 'While now central to the contemporary global economy and the reproduction of global production networks, it is only quite recently that _________ has been more than a marginal influence on patterns of sales and production. The formation of modern _________ was intimately bound up with the emergence of new forms of monopoly capitalism around the end of the 19th and beginning of the 20th century as one element in corporate strategies to create, organize and where possible control markets, especially for mass produced consumer goods.

a. ADTECH
b. Advertising
c. ACNielsen
d. AMAX

49. _________ or _________ data refers to selected population characteristics as used in government, marketing or opinion research, or the _________ profiles used in such research. Note the distinction from the term 'demography' Commonly-used _________ include race, age, income, disabilities, mobility (in terms of travel time to work or number of vehicles available), educational attainment, home ownership, employment status, and even location.

a. African Americans
b. AStore
c. Albert Einstein
d. Demographic

50. _________s are used in open sentences. For instance, in the formula x + 1 = 5, x is a _________ which represents an 'unknown' number. _________s are often represented by letters of the Roman alphabet, or those of other alphabets, such as Greek, and use other special symbols.

a. Variable
b. Book of business
c. Personalization
d. Quantitative

51. The United States _________ is the government agency that is responsible for the United States Census. It also gathers other national demographic and economic data.

a. Census Bureau
b. Power III
c. 6-3-5 Brainwriting
d. 180SearchAssistant

52. A personal and cultural _________ is a relative ethic _________, an assumption upon which implementation can be extrapolated. A _________ system is a set of consistent _________s and measures that is soo not true. A principle _________ is a foundation upon which other _________s and measures of integrity are based.

a. Supreme Court of the United States
b. Package-on-Package
c. Perceptual maps
d. Value

53. _________ is the equation of personal happiness with consumption and the purchase of material possessions.

The term is often associated with criticisms of consumption starting with Thorstein Veblen.

Veblen's subject of examination, the newly emergent middle class arising at the turn of the twentieth century, comes to full fruition by the end of the twentieth century through the process of globalization.

In economics, _________ refers to economic policies placing emphasis on consumption.

a. 180SearchAssistant
b. Power III
c. Consumerism
d. 6-3-5 Brainwriting

1. _________ is defined by the American _________ Association as the activity, set of institutions, and processes for creating, communicating, delivering, and exchanging offerings that have value for customers, clients, partners, and society at large. The term developed from the original meaning which referred literally to going to market, as in shopping, or going to a market to sell goods or services.

_________ practice tends to be seen as a creative industry, which includes advertising, distribution and selling.

a. Product naming
b. Customer acquisition management
c. Marketing myopia
d. Marketing

2. The _________ is a marketing term and refers to all of the forces outside of marketing that affect marketing management's ability to build and maintain successful relationships with target customers. The _________ consists of both the macroenvironment and the microenvironment.

The microenvironment refers to the forces that are close to the company and affect its ability to serve its customers.

a. Psychographic
b. Business-to-consumer
c. Market environment
d. Customer franchise

3. _________ refers to a type of marketing involving the cooperative efforts of a 'for profit' business and a non-profit organization for mutual benefit. The term is sometimes used more broadly and generally to refer to any type of marketing effort for social and other charitable causes, including in-house marketing efforts by non-profit organizations. Cause marketing differs from corporate giving (philanthropy) as the latter generally involves a specific donation that is tax deductible, while cause marketing is a marketing relationship generally not based on a donation.

a. Digital marketing
b. Global marketing
c. Diversity marketing
d. Cause-related marketing

4. According to the American Marketing Association, _________ is the marketing of products that are presumed to be environmentally safe. Thus _________ incorporates a broad range of activities, including product modification, changes to the production process, packaging changes, as well as modifying advertising. Yet defining _________ is not a simple task where several meanings intersect and contradict each other; an example of this will be the existence of varying social, environmental and retail definitions attached to this term.

a. Customer Interaction Tracker
b. Commercialization
c. Value proposition
d. Green marketing

5. _________ is the equation of personal happiness with consumption and the purchase of material possessions.

The term is often associated with criticisms of consumption starting with Thorstein Veblen.

Veblen's subject of examination, the newly emergent middle class arising at the turn of the twentieth century, comes to full fruition by the end of the twentieth century through the process of globalization.

In economics, _________ refers to economic policies placing emphasis on consumption.

a. 180SearchAssistant
b. Consumerism
c. Power III
d. 6-3-5 Brainwriting

6. _________ is a branch of philosophy which seeks to address questions about morality, such as how a moral outcome can be achieved in a specific situation (applied _________), how moral values should be determined (normative _________), what moral values people actually abide by (descriptive _________), what the fundamental semantic, ontological, and epistemic nature of _________ or morality is (meta-_________), and how moral capacity or moral agency develops and what its nature is (moral psychology.)

Socrates was one of the first Greek philosophers to encourage both scholars and the common citizen to turn their attention from the outside world to the condition of man. In this view, Knowledge having a bearing on human life was placed highest, all other knowledge being secondary.

a. AMAX
b. ADTECH
c. ACNielsen
d. Ethics

7. _________ can be regarded as an outcome of mental processes (cognitive process) leading to the selection of a course of action among several alternatives. Every _________ process produces a final choice. The output can be an action or an opinion of choice.

a. 180SearchAssistant
b. Power III
c. Decision making
d. 6-3-5 Brainwriting

8. _________ is one of the four Ps of the marketing mix. The other three aspects are product, promotion, and place. It is also a key variable in microeconomic price allocation theory.

a. Pricing
b. Price
c. Competitor indexing
d. Relationship based pricing

9. Organizational culture is not the same as _________. It is wider and deeper concepts, something that an organization 'is' rather than what it 'has' (according to Buchanan and Huczynski.)

_________ is the total sum of the values, customs, traditions and meanings that make a company unique.

a. Corporate culture
b. Power III
c. Cross-functional team
d. 180SearchAssistant

10. _________ is difficult to define. For example, in 1952, Alfred Kroeber and Clyde Kluckhohn compiled a list of 164 definitions of '_________' in _________: A Critical Review of Concepts and Definitions. However, the word '_________' is most commonly used in three basic senses:

- excellence of taste in the fine arts and humanities
- an integrated pattern of human knowledge, belief, and behavior that depends upon the capacity for symbolic thought and social learning
- the set of shared attitudes, values, goals, and practices that characterizes an institution, organization or group.

When the concept first emerged in eighteenth- and nineteenth-century Europe, it connoted a process of cultivation or improvement, as in agriculture or horticulture. In the nineteenth century, it came to refer first to the betterment or refinement of the individual, especially through education, and then to the fulfillment of national aspirations or ideals.

a. Albert Einstein
b. African Americans
c. AStore
d. Culture

11. _________ is an organization's process of defining its strategy and making decisions on allocating its resources to pursue this strategy, including its capital and people. Various business analysis techniques can be used in _________, including SWOT analysis (Strengths, Weaknesses, Opportunities, and Threats) and PEST analysis (Political, Economic, Social, and Technological analysis) or STEER analysis involving Socio-cultural, Technological, Economic, Ecological, and Regulatory factors and EPISTEL (Environment, Political, Informatic, Social, Technological, Economic and Legal)

_________ is the formal consideration of an organization's future course. All _________ deals with at least one of three key questions:

1. 'What do we do?'
2. 'For whom do we do it?'
3. 'How do we excel?'

In business _________, the third question is better phrased 'How can we beat or avoid competition?'. (Bradford and Duncan, page 1.)

a. Power III
b. Strategic planning
c. 6-3-5 Brainwriting
d. 180SearchAssistant

12. _________ in organizations and public policy is both the organizational process of creating and maintaining a plan; and the psychological process of thinking about the activities required to create a desired goal on some scale. As such, it is a fundamental property of intelligent behavior. This thought process is essential to the creation and refinement of a plan, or integration of it with other plans, that is, it combines forecasting of developments with the preparation of scenarios of how to react to them.

a. 180SearchAssistant
b. Power III
c. 6-3-5 Brainwriting
d. Planning

1. The Oxford University Press defines _________ as 'marketing on a worldwide scale reconciling or taking commercial advantage of global operational differences, similarities and opportunities in order to meet global objectives.' Oxford University Press' Glossary of Marketing Terms.

Here are three reasons for the shift from domestic to _________ as given by the authors of the textbook, _________ Management--3rd Edition by Masaaki Kotabe and Kristiaan Helsen, 2004.

One of the product categories in which global competition has been easy to track is in U.S. automotive sales.

a. Guerrilla Marketing
b. Digital marketing
c. Diversity marketing
d. Global marketing

2. _________ is defined by the American _________ Association as the activity, set of institutions, and processes for creating, communicating, delivering, and exchanging offerings that have value for customers, clients, partners, and society at large. The term developed from the original meaning which referred literally to going to market, as in shopping, or going to a market to sell goods or services.

_________ practice tends to be seen as a creative industry, which includes advertising, distribution and selling.

a. Product naming
b. Marketing myopia
c. Marketing
d. Customer acquisition management

3. _________, also referred to as i-marketing, web marketing, online marketing is the marketing of products or services over the Internet.

The Internet has brought many unique benefits to marketing, one of which being lower costs for the distribution of information and media to a global audience. The interactive nature of _________, both in terms of providing instant response and eliciting responses, is a unique quality of the medium.

a. ACNielsen
b. AMAX
c. ADTECH
d. Internet marketing

4. _________ is the identity of a group or culture, or of an individual as far as one is influenced by one's belonging to a group or culture. _________ is similar to and has overlaps with, but is not synonymous with, identity politics.

There are modern questions of culture that are transferred into questions of identity.

a. 180SearchAssistant
b. 6-3-5 Brainwriting
c. Power III
d. Cultural identity

5. The _________ is a marketing term and refers to all of the forces outside of marketing that affect marketing management's ability to build and maintain successful relationships with target customers. The _________ consists of both the macroenvironment and the microenvironment.

The microenvironment refers to the forces that are close to the company and affect its ability to serve its customers.

a. Market environment
b. Business-to-consumer
c. Customer franchise
d. Psychographic

6. _________ is a branch of philosophy which seeks to address questions about morality, such as how a moral outcome can be achieved in a specific situation (applied _________), how moral values should be determined (normative _________), what moral values people actually abide by (descriptive _________), what the fundamental semantic, ontological, and epistemic nature of _________ or morality is (meta-_________), and how moral capacity or moral agency develops and what its nature is (moral psychology.)

Socrates was one of the first Greek philosophers to encourage both scholars and the common citizen to turn their attention from the outside world to the condition of man. In this view, Knowledge having a bearing on human life was placed highest, all other knowledge being secondary.

a. ACNielsen
b. AMAX
c. ADTECH
d. Ethics

7. _________s is the social science that studies the production, distribution, and consumption of goods and services. The term _________s comes from the Ancient Greek oá¼°κονομΐ¯α from oá¼¶κος (oikos, 'house') + vÏŒμος (nomos, 'custom' or 'law'), hence 'rules of the house(hold)'. Current _________ models developed out of the broader field of political economy in the late 19th century, owing to a desire to use an empirical approach more akin to the physical sciences.

a. Economic
b. ACNielsen
c. Industrial organization
d. ADTECH

8. The _________ is the difference between the monetary value of exports and imports in an economy over a certain period of time. It is the relationship between a nation's imports and exports. A positive _________ is known as a trade surplus and consists of exporting more than is imported; a negative _________ is known as a trade deficit or, informally, a trade gap.

a. Value added
b. Balance of trade
c. Deregulation
d. Power III

9. _________ are various forms of controls imposed by a government on the purchase/sale of foreign currencies by residents or on the purchase/sale of local currency by nonresidents.

Common _________ include:

- Banning the use of foreign currency within the country
- Banning locals from possessing foreign currency
- Restricting currency exchange to government-approved exchangers
- Fixed exchange rates
- Restrictions on the amount of currency that may be imported or exported

Countries with _________ are also known as 'Article 14 countries,' after the provision in the International Monetary Fund agreement allowing exchange controls for transitional economies. Such controls used to be common in most countries, particularly poorer ones, until the 1990s when free trade and globalization started a trend towards economic liberalization. Today, countries which still impose exchange controls are the exception rather than the rule.

a. 6-3-5 Brainwriting
b. Foreign exchange controls
c. Power III
d. 180SearchAssistant

10. The _________ or gross domestic income (GDI) is one of the measures of national income and output for a given country's economy. It is the total value of all final goods and services produced in a particular economy; the dollar value of all goods and services produced within a country's borders in a given year. _________ can be defined in three ways, all of which are conceptually identical.

a. Macroeconomics
b. Leading indicator
c. Microeconomics
d. Gross domestic product

11. A _________ is a tax imposed on goods when they are moved across a political boundary. They are usually associated with protectionism, the economic policy of restraining trade between nations. For political reasons, _________s are usually imposed on imported goods, although they may also be imposed on exported goods.

a. Tariff
b. Power III
c. Fiscal policy
d. Monetary policy

12. The _________ is a trilateral trade bloc in North America created by the governments of the United States, Canada, and Mexico. It superseded the Canada-United States Free Trade Agreement between the US and Canada.

Following diplomatic negotiations dating back to 1990 between the three nations, the leaders met in San Antonio, Texas on December 17, 1992 to sign _________.

a. 6-3-5 Brainwriting
b. Power III
c. 180SearchAssistant
d. North American Free Trade Agreement

13. A _________ is a customs union with common policies on product regulation, and freedom of movement of the factors of production (capital and labour) and of enterprise. The goal is that the movement of capital, labour, goods, and services between the members is as easy as within them. This is the fourth stage of economic integration.

a. Monetary union
b. Customs union
c. Competitive
d. Common Market

14. The _________ is an economic and political union of 27 member states, located primarily in Europe. It was established by the Treaty of Maastricht on 1 November 1993 upon the foundations of the pre-existing European Economic Community. With almost 500 million citizens, the _________ combined generates an estimated 30% share (US$16.8 trillion in 2007) of the nominal gross world product.

a. Eurozone
b. ACNielsen
c. ADTECH
d. European Union

15. A _________ or maquila is a factory that imports materials and equipment on a duty-free and tariff-free basis for assembly or manufacturing and then re-exports the assembled product, usually back to the originating country. A maquila is also referred to as a 'twin plant', or 'in-bond' industry. Nearly half a million Mexicans are employed in _________s.

a. 6-3-5 Brainwriting
b. Power III
c. 180SearchAssistant
d. Maquiladora

16. In economics, '_________' can refer to any kind of predatory pricing. However, the word is now generally used only in the context of international trade law, where _________ is defined as the act of a manufacturer in one country exporting a product to another country at a price which is either below the price it charges in its home market or is below its costs of production. The term has a negative connotation, but advocates of free markets see '_________' as beneficial for consumers and believe that protectionism to prevent it would have net negative consequences.

a. Hawkers
b. Gold Key Matching Service
c. Sample sales
d. Dumping

17. The _________ was the outcome of the failure of negotiating governments to create the International Trade Organization (ITO.) GATT was formed in 1947 and lasted until 1994, when it was replaced by the World Trade Organization. The Bretton Woods Conference had introduced the idea for an organization to regulate trade as part of a larger plan for economic recovery after World War II.

a. General Agreement on Tariffs and Trade
b. Trade pact
c. Power III
d. General Agreement on Trade in Services

18. The _________ is an international organization designed to supervise and liberalize international trade. The _________ came into being on 1 January 1995, and is the successor to the General Agreement on Tariffs and Trade (GATT), which was created in 1947, and continued to operate for almost five decades as a de facto international organization.

The _________ deals with the rules of trade between nations at a near-global level; it is responsible for negotiating and implementing new trade agreements, and is in charge of policing member countries' adherence to all the _________ agreements, signed by the majority of the world's trading nations and ratified in their parliaments.

a. Merchandise Mart
b. Population Reference Bureau
c. World Trade Organization
d. BSI Group

19. _________ is a broad label that refers to any individuals or households that use goods and services generated within the economy. The concept of a _________ is used in different contexts, so that the usage and significance of the term may vary.

A _________ is a person who uses any product or service.

a. Consumer
b. 6-3-5 Brainwriting
c. Power III
d. 180SearchAssistant

20. _________ is exchange of capital, goods, and services across international borders or territories. In most countries, it represents a significant share of gross domestic product (GDP.) While _________ has been present throughout much of history , its economic, social, and political importance has been on the rise in recent centuries.

a. International trade
b. ADTECH
c. Incoterms
d. ACNielsen

21. The verb _________ or grant _________ means to give permission. The noun _________ refers to that permission as well as to the document memorializing that permission. _________ may be granted by a party to another party as an element of an agreement between those parties.

a. 6-3-5 Brainwriting
b. License
c. Power III
d. 180SearchAssistant

22. A _________ is a firm that manufactures components or products for another 'hiring' firm. Many industries utilize this process, especially the aerospace, defense, computer, semiconductor, energy, medical, food manufacturing, personal care, and automotive fields. Some types of contract manufacturing include CNC machining, complex assembly, aluminum die casting, grinding, broaching, gears, and forging.
a. Power III
b. Productivity
c. 180SearchAssistant
d. Contract manufacturer

23. _________ refers to the methods of practicing and using another person's philosophy of business. The franchisor grants the independent operator the right to distribute its products, techniques, and trademarks for a percentage of gross monthly sales and a royalty fee. Various tangibles and intangibles such as national or international advertising, training, and other support services are commonly made available by the franchisor.
a. 180SearchAssistant
b. Franchising
c. Franchise fee
d. Power III

24. A _________ is an entity formed between two or more parties to undertake economic activity together. The parties agree to create a new entity by both contributing equity, and they then share in the revenues, expenses, and control of the enterprise. The venture can be for one specific project only, or a continuing business relationship such as the Fuji Xerox _________.
a. Gripe site
b. Consumer protection
c. Trademark attorney
d. Joint venture

25. _________ is the state or fact of exclusive rights and control over property, which may be an object, land/real estate, or some other kind of property (like government-granted monopolies collectively referred to as intellectual property.) It is embodied in an _________ right also referred to as title.

_________ is the key building block in the development of the capitalist socio-economic system.

a. AMAX
b. ACNielsen
c. Ownership
d. ADTECH

26. On an intranet or B2E Enterprise Web portals, personalization is often based on user attributes such as department, functional area, or role. The term _________ in this context refers to the ability of users to modify the page layout or specify what content should be displayed.

There are two categories of personalizations:

1. Rule-based
2. Content-based

Web personalization models include rules-based filtering, based on 'if this, then that' rules processing, and collaborative filtering, which serves relevant material to customers by combining their own personal preferences with the preferences of like-minded others. Collaborative filtering works well for books, music, video, etc.

a. Self branding
b. Movin'
c. Cashmere Agency
d. Customization

27. _________ in its literal sense is the process of transformation of local or regional phenomena into global ones. It can be described as a process by which the people of the world are unified into a single society and function together.

This process is a combination of economic, technological, sociocultural and political forces.

a. Power III
b. Globalization
c. 6-3-5 Brainwriting
d. 180SearchAssistant

28. A _________ is a process that can allow an organization to concentrate its limited resources on the greatest opportunities to increase sales and achieve a sustainable competitive advantage. A _________ should be centered around the key concept that customer satisfaction is the main goal.

A _________ is most effective when it is an integral component of corporate strategy, defining how the organization will successfully engage customers, prospects, and competitors in the market arena.

a. Societal marketing
b. Cyberdoc
c. Marketing strategy
d. Psychographic

1. _________ is defined by the American _________ Association as the activity, set of institutions, and processes for creating, communicating, delivering, and exchanging offerings that have value for customers, clients, partners, and society at large. The term developed from the original meaning which referred literally to going to market, as in shopping, or going to a market to sell goods or services.

_________ practice tends to be seen as a creative industry, which includes advertising, distribution and selling.

a. Customer acquisition management
b. Marketing
c. Product naming
d. Marketing myopia

2. Consumer market research is a form of applied sociology that concentrates on understanding the behaviours, whims and preferences, of consumers in a market-based economy, and aims to understand the effects and comparative success of marketing campaigns. The field of consumer _________ as a statistical science was pioneered by Arthur Nielsen with the founding of the ACNielsen Company in 1923 .

Thus _________ is the systematic and objective identification, collection, analysis, and dissemination of information for the purpose of assisting management in decision making related to the identification and solution of problems and opportunities in marketing.

a. Marketing research process
b. Focus group
c. Logit analysis
d. Marketing research

3. A number of different _________s are indicated below.

- Randomized controlled trial
  - Double-blind randomized trial
  - Single-blind randomized trial
  - Non-blind trial
- Nonrandomized trial (quasi-experiment)
  - Interrupted time series design (measures on a sample or a series of samples from the same population are obtained several times before and after a manipulated event or a naturally occurring event) - considered a type of quasi-experiment

- Cohort study
  - Prospective cohort
  - Retrospective cohort
  - Time series study
- Case-control study
  - Nested case-control study
- Cross-sectional study
  - Community survey (a type of cross-sectional study)

When choosing a _________, many factors must be taken into account. Different types of studies are subject to different types of bias. For example, recall bias is likely to occur in cross-sectional or case-control studies where subjects are asked to recall exposure to risk factors.

a. Longitudinal studies
b. Power III
c. 180SearchAssistant
d. Study design

4. _________ refer to a collection of facts usually collected as the result of experience, observation or experiment or a set of premises. This may consist of numbers, words particularly as measurements or observations of a set of variables. _________ are often viewed as a lowest level of abstraction from which information and knowledge are derived.

a. Pearson product-moment correlation coefficient
b. Sample size
c. Mean
d. Data

5. _________ is a term used to describe a process of preparing and collecting data - for example as part of a process improvement or similar project.

_________ usually takes place early on in an improvement project, and is often formalised through a _________ Plan which often contains the following activity.

1. Pre collection activity - Agree goals, target data, definitions, methods
2. Collection - _________
3. Present Findings - usually involves some form of sorting analysis and/or presentation.

A formal _________ process is necessary as it ensures that data gathered is both defined and accurate and that subsequent decisions based on arguments embodied in the findings are valid . The process provides both a baseline from which to measure from and in certain cases a target on what to improve. Types of _________ 1-By mail questionnaires 2-By personal interview

- Six sigma
- Sampling (statistics)

.

a. 180SearchAssistant
b. 6-3-5 Brainwriting
c. Data collection
d. Power III

6. _________ describes data and characteristics about the population or phenomenon being studied. _________ answers the questions who, what, where, when and how.

Although the data description is factual, accurate and systematic, the research cannot describe what caused a situation.

a. Sampling error
b. Descriptive research
c. Power III
d. Two-tailed test

7. _________ is a type of research conducted because a problem has not been clearly defined. _________ helps determine the best research design, data collection method and selection of subjects. Given its fundamental nature, _________ often concludes that a perceived problem does not actually exist.

a. ACNielsen
b. Exploratory research
c. IDDEA
d. Intent scale translation

8. _________ is a term for unprocessed data, it is also known as primary data. It is a relative term _________ can be input to a computer program or used in manual analysis procedures such as gathering statistics from a survey.

a. Product manager
b. Chief marketing officer
c. Shoppers Food ' Pharmacy
d. Raw data

9. Combining Existing _________ Sources with New Primary Data Sources

Imagine that we could get hold of a good collection of surveys taken in earlier years, such as detailed studies about changes going on in this phase and hopefully additional studies in the years to come. Analyzing this data base over time could give us a good picture of what changes actually have taken place in the orientation of the population and of the extent to which new technical concepts did have an impact on subgroups of the population. Furthermore, data archives can help to prepare studies on change over time by monitoring what questions have been asked in earlier years and alerting principal investigators to important questions which should be repeated in planned research projects.

a. 180SearchAssistant
b. 6-3-5 Brainwriting
c. Secondary data
d. Power III

10. _________ is a way of expressing knowledge or belief that an event will occur or has occurred. In mathematics the concept has been given an exact meaning in _________ theory, that is used extensively in such areas of study as mathematics, statistics, finance, gambling, science, and philosophy to draw conclusions about the likelihood of potential events and the underlying mechanics of complex systems.

a. Data
b. Linear regression
c. Probability
d. Heteroskedastic

11. _________ is that part of statistical practice concerned with the selection of individual observations intended to yield some knowledge about a population of concern, especially for the purposes of statistical inference. Each observation measures one or more properties (weight, location, etc.) of an observable entity enumerated to distinguish objects or individuals.

a. Sports Marketing Group
b. AStore
c. Sampling
d. Richard Buckminster 'Bucky' Fuller

12. _________ is one of the four Ps of the marketing mix. The other three aspects are product, promotion, and place. It is also a key variable in microeconomic price allocation theory.

a. Relationship based pricing
b. Competitor indexing
c. Price
d. Pricing

13. Sampling is the use of a subset of the population to represent the whole population. Probability sampling, or random sampling, is a sampling technique in which the probability of getting any particular sample may be calculated. _________ does not meet this criterion and should be used with caution.

a. Nonprobability sampling
b. Quota sampling
c. Power III
d. Snowball sampling

14. In _________, the population is first segmented into mutually exclusive sub-groups, just as in stratified sampling. Then judgment is used to select the subjects or units from each segment based on a specified proportion. For example, an interviewer may be told to sample 200 females and 300 males between the age of 45 and 60.

a. Nonprobability sampling
b. Power III
c. Snowball sampling
d. Quota sampling

15. _________ are used to collect quantitative information about items in a population. Surveys of human populations and institutions are common in political polling and government, health, social science and marketing research. A survey may focus on opinions or factual information depending on its purpose, and many surveys involve administering questions to individuals.

a. Statistical surveys
b. Convergent
c. BeyondROI
d. Gross Margin Return on Inventory Investment

16. _________ is the examining of goods or services from retailers with the intent to purchase at that time. _________ is an activity of selection and/or purchase. In some contexts it is considered a leisure activity as well as an economic one.

a. Khodebshchik
b. Discount store
c. Hawkers
d. Shopping

17. _________ is a sales technique in which a salesperson walks from one door of a house to another trying to sell a product or service to the general public. A variant of this involves cold calling first, when another sales representative attempts to gain agreement that a salesperson should visit. _________ selling is usually conducted in the afternoon hours, when the majority of people are at home.

a. Marketing management
b. Performance-based advertising
c. Fast moving consumer goods
d. Door-to-door

18. _________ a research method involving the use of questionnaires and/or statistical surveys to gather data about people and their thoughts and behaviours.

a. Z-test
b. Control chart
c. Survey research
d. T-test

19. _________ is a form of assessment in which respondents are asked to select one or more choices from a list. The _________ format is most frequently used in educational testing, in market research, and in elections-- when a person chooses between multiple candidates, parties, or policies. _________ testing is particularly popular in the United States.

a. Multiple choice
b. 180SearchAssistant
c. Power III
d. 6-3-5 Brainwriting

20. _________ is either an activity of a living being (such as a human), consisting of receiving knowledge of the outside world through the senses, or the recording of data using scientific instruments. The term may also refer to any datum collected during this activity.

The scientific method requires _________s of nature to formulate and test hypotheses.

a. ACNielsen
b. ADTECH
c. Observation
d. AMAX

21. A _________ is a research instrument consisting of a series of questions and other prompts for the purpose of gathering information from respondents. Although they are often designed for statistical analysis of the responses, this is not always the case. The _________ was invented by Sir Francis Galton.

a. Market research
b. Mystery shoppers
c. Mystery shopping
d. Questionnaire

22. _________ in economics and business is the result of an exchange and from that trade we assign a numerical monetary value to a good, service or asset. If I trade 4 apples for an orange, the _________ of an orange is 4 - apples. Inversely, the _________ of an apple is 1/4 oranges.

a. Contribution margin-based pricing
b. Price
c. Discounts and allowances
d. Pricing

23. A _________ is a structured collection of records or data that is stored in a computer system. The structure is achieved by organizing the data according to a _________ model. The model in most common use today is the relational model.

a. Power III
b. 180SearchAssistant
c. 6-3-5 Brainwriting
d. Database

24. _________ is the process of extracting hidden patterns from data. As more data is gathered, with the amount of data doubling every three years, _________ is becoming an increasingly important tool to transform this data into information. It is commonly used in a wide range of profiling practices, such as marketing, surveillance, fraud detection and scientific discovery.

a. 180SearchAssistant
b. Data mining
c. Structure mining
d. Power III

25. _________ is an information system that helps with decision-making in the formation of a marketing plan. The reason for using an MKDSS is because it helps to support the software vendors' planning strategy for marketing products; it can help to identify advantageous levels of pricing, advertising spending, and advertising copy for the firm's products (Arinze, 1990.) This helps determines the firms marketing mix for product software.

a. 6-3-5 Brainwriting
b. 180SearchAssistant
c. Power III
d. Marketing decision support systems

26. An _________ is a market form in which a market or industry is dominated by a small number of sellers (oligopolists.) Because there are few participants in this type of market, each oligopolist is aware of the actions of the others. The decisions of one firm influence, and are influenced by, the decisions of other firms.

a. ADTECH
b. AMAX
c. ACNielsen
d. Oligopoly

27. _________ constitute a class of computer-based information systems including knowledge-based systems that support decision-making activities.

_________ are a specific class of computerized information system that supports business and organizational decision-making activities. A properly-designed _________ is an interactive software-based system intended to help decision makers compile useful information from raw data, documents, personal knowledge, and/or business models to identify and solve problems and make decisions.

a. 6-3-5 Brainwriting
b. Decision support systems
c. 180SearchAssistant
d. Power III

28. The Oxford University Press defines _________ as 'marketing on a worldwide scale reconciling or taking commercial advantage of global operational differences, similarities and opportunities in order to meet global objectives.' Oxford University Press' Glossary of Marketing Terms.

Here are three reasons for the shift from domestic to _________ as given by the authors of the textbook, _________ Management--3rd Edition by Masaaki Kotabe and Kristiaan Helsen, 2004.

One of the product categories in which global competition has been easy to track is in U.S. automotive sales.

a. Guerrilla Marketing
b. Digital marketing
c. Global marketing
d. Diversity marketing

29. The _________ is a marketing term and refers to all of the forces outside of marketing that affect marketing management's ability to build and maintain successful relationships with target customers. The _________ consists of both the macroenvironment and the microenvironment.

The microenvironment refers to the forces that are close to the company and affect its ability to serve its customers.

a. Customer franchise
b. Market environment
c. Psychographic
d. Business-to-consumer

30. _________, also referred to as i-marketing, web marketing, online marketing is the marketing of products or services over the Internet.

The Internet has brought many unique benefits to marketing, one of which being lower costs for the distribution of information and media to a global audience. The interactive nature of _________, both in terms of providing instant response and eliciting responses, is a unique quality of the medium.

a. Internet marketing
b. AMAX
c. ACNielsen
d. ADTECH

1. _________ is a broad label that refers to any individuals or households that use goods and services generated within the economy. The concept of a _________ is used in different contexts, so that the usage and significance of the term may vary.

A _________ is a person who uses any product or service.

a. Power III
b. Consumer
c. 6-3-5 Brainwriting
d. 180SearchAssistant

2. _________ is a business term meaning the market segment to which a particular good or service is marketed. It is mainly defined by age, gender, geography, socio-economic grouping, technographic, or any other combination of demographics. It is generally studied and mapped by an organization through lists and reports containing demographic information that may have an effect on the marketing of key products or services.

a. Distribution
b. Category Development Index
c. Brando
d. Market specialization

3. A _________ is a plan of action designed to achieve a particular goal.

_________ is different from tactics. In military terms, tactics is concerned with the conduct of an engagement while _________ is concerned with how different engagements are linked.

a. Power III
b. Strategy
c. 6-3-5 Brainwriting
d. 180SearchAssistant

4. A _________ is a subgroup of people or organizations sharing one or more characteristics that cause them to have similar product and/or service needs. A true _________ meets all of the following criteria: it is distinct from other segments (different segments have different needs), it is homogeneous within the segment (exhibits common needs); it responds similarly to a market stimulus, and it can be reached by a market intervention. The term is also used when consumers with identical product and/or service needs are divided up into groups so they can be charged different amounts.

a. Market segment
b. Commercial planning
c. Production orientation
d. Customer insight

5. _________ or _________ data refers to selected population characteristics as used in government, marketing or opinion research, or the _________ profiles used in such research. Note the distinction from the term 'demography' Commonly-used _________ include race, age, income, disabilities, mobility (in terms of travel time to work or number of vehicles available), educational attainment, home ownership, employment status, and even location.

a. African Americans
b. AStore
c. Albert Einstein
d. Demographic

6. _________ is defined by the American _________ Association as the activity, set of institutions, and processes for creating, communicating, delivering, and exchanging offerings that have value for customers, clients, partners, and society at large. The term developed from the original meaning which referred literally to going to market, as in shopping, or going to a market to sell goods or services.

_________ practice tends to be seen as a creative industry, which includes advertising, distribution and selling.

a. Product naming
b. Customer acquisition management
c. Marketing myopia
d. Marketing

7. The _________ is a marketing term and refers to all of the forces outside of marketing that affect marketing management's ability to build and maintain successful relationships with target customers. The _________ consists of both the macroenvironment and the microenvironment.

The microenvironment refers to the forces that are close to the company and affect its ability to serve its customers.

a. Psychographic
b. Business-to-consumer
c. Customer franchise
d. Market environment

8. _________s are used in open sentences. For instance, in the formula x + 1 = 5, x is a _________ which represents an 'unknown' number. _________s are often represented by letters of the Roman alphabet, or those of other alphabets, such as Greek, and use other special symbols.

a. Book of business
b. Variable
c. Personalization
d. Quantitative

9. The Oxford University Press defines _________ as 'marketing on a worldwide scale reconciling or taking commercial advantage of global operational differences, similarities and opportunities in order to meet global objectives.' Oxford University Press' Glossary of Marketing Terms.

Here are three reasons for the shift from domestic to _________ as given by the authors of the textbook, _________ Management--3rd Edition by Masaaki Kotabe and Kristiaan Helsen, 2004.

One of the product categories in which global competition has been easy to track is in U.S. automotive sales.

a. Diversity marketing
b. Digital marketing
c. Guerrilla Marketing
d. Global marketing

10. _________, also referred to as i-marketing, web marketing, online marketing is the marketing of products or services over the Internet.

The Internet has brought many unique benefits to marketing, one of which being lower costs for the distribution of information and media to a global audience. The interactive nature of _________, both in terms of providing instant response and eliciting responses, is a unique quality of the medium.

a. ADTECH
b. AMAX
c. Internet marketing
d. ACNielsen

11. _________ is the study of the Earth and its lands, features, inhabitants, and phenomena. A literal translation would be 'to describe or write about the Earth'. The first person to use the word '_________' was Eratosthenes .

a. Power III
b. 180SearchAssistant
c. Geography
d. 6-3-5 Brainwriting

12. Its a tool for marketing. _________ is a multivariate statistical classification technique for discovering whether the individuals of a population fall into different groups by making quantitative comparisons of multiple characteristics with the assumption that the differences within any group should be less than the differences between groups.

The information technologies employed in _________ include geographic information system and database management software.

a. Geodemographic segmentation
b. Principal component analysis
c. Linear discriminant analysis
d. Multiple discriminant analysis

13. _________ is the practice of tailoring products, brands (microbrands), and promotions to meet the needs and wants of microsegments within a market. It is a type of market customization that deals with pricing of customer/product combinations at the store or individual level.

Standard pricing policy ignores the differences in customer segments of specific stores within a regional chain of stores.

a. Micromarketing
b. Chief privacy officer
c. Discontinuation
d. Soft sell

14. In the field of marketing, demographics, opinion research, and social research in general, _________ variables are any attributes relating to personality, values, attitudes, interests, or lifestyles. They are also called IAO variables . They can be contrasted with demographic variables (such as age and gender), behavioral variables (such as usage rate or loyalty), and bizographic variables (such as industry, seniority and functional area.)

a. Lifetime value
b. Psychographic
c. Marketing myopia
d. Business-to-business

15. _________ in economics and business is the result of an exchange and from that trade we assign a numerical monetary value to a good, service or asset. If I trade 4 apples for an orange, the _________ of an orange is 4 - apples. Inversely, the _________ of an apple is 1/4 oranges.

a. Pricing
b. Discounts and allowances
c. Contribution margin-based pricing
d. Price

16. _________ is a strategic planning method used to evaluate the Strengths, Weaknesses, Opportunities, and Threats involved in a project or in a business venture. It involves specifying the objective of the business venture or project and identifying the internal and external factors that are favorable and unfavorable to achieving that objective. The technique is credited to Albert Humphrey, who led a research project at Stanford University in the 1960s and 1970s using data from Fortune 500 companies.

a. SWOT analysis
b. Product differentiation
c. Market environment
d. Lead scoring

17. _________ involves disseminating information about a product, product line, brand, or company. It is one of the four key aspects of the marketing mix. (The other three elements are product marketing, pricing, and distribution). P>_________ is generally sub-divided into two parts:

- Above the line _________: Promotion in the media (e.g. TV, radio, newspapers, Internet and Mobile Phones) in which the advertiser pays an advertising agency to place the ad
- Below the line _________: All other _________. Much of this is intended to be subtle enough for the consumer to be unaware that _________ is taking place. E.g. sponsorship, product placement, endorsements, sales _________, merchandising, direct mail, personal selling, public relations, trade shows

a. Davie Brown Index b. Cashmere Agency
c. Promotion d. Bottling lines

18. _________ is systematic determination of merit, worth, and significance of something or someone using criteria against a set of standards. _________ often is used to characterize and appraise subjects of interest in a wide range of human enterprises, including the arts, criminal justice, foundations and non-profit organizations, government, health care, and other human services.

Depending on the topic of interest, there are professional groups which look to the quality and rigor of the _________ process.

a. ADTECH b. Evaluation
c. ACNielsen d. AMAX

19. _________ is a rivalry between individuals, groups, nations for territory, a niche, or allocation of resources. It arises whenever two or more parties strive for a goal which cannot be shared. _________ occurs naturally between living organisms which co-exist in the same environment.

a. Competition b. Price fixing
c. Price competition d. Non-price competition

20. In economics, business, retail, and accounting, a _________ is the value of money that has been used up to produce something, and hence is not available for use anymore. In economics, a _________ is an alternative that is given up as a result of a decision. In business, the _________ may be one of acquisition, in which case the amount of money expended to acquire it is counted as _________.

a. Fixed costs b. Variable cost
c. Cost d. Transaction cost

21. The break-even point for a product is the point where total revenue received equals the total costs associated with the sale of the product (TR=TC.) A break-even point is typically calculated in order for businesses to determine if it would be profitable to sell a proposed product, as opposed to attempting to modify an existing product instead so it can be made lucrative. _________ can also be used to analyse the potential profitability of an expenditure in a sales-based business.

In _________, margin of safety is how much output or sales level can fall before a business reaches its break-even point (BEP).

a. Price skimming
b. Contribution margin-based pricing
c. Pay Per Sale
d. Break even analysis

22. _________ is the process of estimation in unknown situations. Prediction is a similar, but more general term. Both can refer to estimation of time series, cross-sectional or longitudinal data.

a. Power III
b. 180SearchAssistant
c. Forecasting
d. 6-3-5 Brainwriting

23. In statistics, _________ is a collective name for techniques for the modeling and analysis of numerical data consisting of values of a dependent variable and of one or more independent variables The dependent variable in the regression equation is modeled as a function of the independent variables, corresponding parameters, and an error term. The error term is treated as a random variable.

a. Multicollinearity
b. Regression analysis
c. Variance inflation factor
d. Stepwise regression

24. _________ is a statistical method used to describe variability among observed variables in terms of fewer unobserved variables called factors. The observed variables are modeled as linear combinations of the factors, plus 'error' terms. The information gained about the interdependencies can be used later to reduce the set of variables in a dataset.

a. Likert scale
b. Power III
c. Factor analysis
d. Semantic differential

1. _________ is a broad label that refers to any individuals or households that use goods and services generated within the economy. The concept of a _________ is used in different contexts, so that the usage and significance of the term may vary.

A _________ is a person who uses any product or service.

a. Consumer
b. 6-3-5 Brainwriting
c. Power III
d. 180SearchAssistant

2. An _________ is an unplanned or otherwise spontaneous purchase. One who tends to make such purchases is referred to as an impulse purchaser or impulse buyer.

Marketers and retailers tend to exploit these impulses which are tied to the basic want for instant gratification.

a. ACNielsen
b. ADTECH
c. AMAX
d. Impulse purchase

3. _________ is systematic determination of merit, worth, and significance of something or someone using criteria against a set of standards. _________ often is used to characterize and appraise subjects of interest in a wide range of human enterprises, including the arts, criminal justice, foundations and non-profit organizations, government, health care, and other human services.

Depending on the topic of interest, there are professional groups which look to the quality and rigor of the _________ process.

a. ACNielsen
b. Evaluation
c. AMAX
d. ADTECH

4. In economics, an externality or spillover of an economic transaction is an impact on a party that is not directly involved in the transaction. In such a case, prices do not reflect the full costs or benefits in production or consumption of a product or service. A positive impact is called an _________ benefit, while a negative impact is called an _________ cost.

a. ADTECH
b. AMAX
c. External
d. ACNielsen

5. _________ is a form of communication that typically attempts to persuade potential customers to purchase or to consume more of a particular brand of product or service. 'While now central to the contemporary global economy and the reproduction of global production networks, it is only quite recently that _________ has been more than a marginal influence on patterns of sales and production. The formation of modern _________ was intimately bound up with the emergence of new forms of monopoly capitalism around the end of the 19th and beginning of the 20th century as one element in corporate strategies to create, organize and where possible control markets, especially for mass produced consumer goods.

a. Advertising
b. AMAX
c. ACNielsen
d. ADTECH

6. Cognition is the scientific term for 'the process of thought.' Its usage varies in different ways in accord with different disciplines: For example, in psychology and _________ science it refers to an information processing view of an individual's psychological functions. Other interpretations of the meaning of cognition link it to the development of concepts; individual minds, groups, organizations, and even larger coalitions of entities, can be modelled as 'societies' (Society of Mind), which cooperate to form concepts.

The autonomous elements of each 'society' would have the opportunity to demonstrate emergent behavior in the face of some crisis or opportunity.

a. Cognitive
b. 6-3-5 Brainwriting
c. Power III
d. 180SearchAssistant

7. _________ is an uncomfortable feeling caused by holding two contradictory ideas simultaneously. The 'ideas' or 'cognitions' in question may include attitudes and beliefs, and also the awareness of one's behavior. The theory of _________ proposes that people have a motivational drive to reduce dissonance by changing their attitudes, beliefs, and behaviors, or by justifying or rationalizing their attitudes, beliefs, and behaviors.

a. Perception
b. Cognitive dissonance
c. Power III
d. 180SearchAssistant

8. In psychology, philosophy, and the cognitive sciences, _________ is the process of attaining awareness or understanding of sensory information. It is a task far more complex than was imagined in the 1950s and 1960s, when it was predicted that building perceiving machines would take about a decade, a goal which is still very far from fruition. The word _________ comes from the Latin words _________, percepio, meaning 'receiving, collecting, action of taking possession, apprehension with the mind or senses.'

_________ is one of the oldest fields in psychology.

a. 180SearchAssistant
b. Power III
c. Groupthink
d. Perception

9. _________ is the process when people remember messages that are closer to their interests, values and beliefs more accurately, than those that are in contrast with their values and beliefs, selecting what to keep in the memory, narrowing the informational flow.

Such examples could include:

- A person may gradually reflect more positively on their time at school as they grow older
- A consumer might remember only the positive health benefits of a product they enjoy
- People tending to omit problems and disputes in past relationships
- A conspiracy theorist paying less attention to facts which do not aid their standpoint

.

a. Power III
b. 180SearchAssistant
c. 6-3-5 Brainwriting
d. Selective retention

10. _________ is a term that refers to the tendency of people to interpret information in a way that will support what they already believe. This concept, along with selective attention and selective retention, makes it hard for marketers to get their message across and create good product perception.

a. 180SearchAssistant
b. Power III
c. Psychological Abstracts
d. Selective distortion

11. _________ consists of the sale of goods or merchandise from a fixed location, such as a department store or kiosk in small or individual lots for direct consumption by the purchaser. _________ may include subordinated services, such as delivery. Purchasers may be individuals or businesses.

a. Charity shop
b. Thrifting
c. Warehouse store
d. Retailing

12. Maslow's _________ is a theory in psychology, proposed by Abraham Maslow in his 1943 paper A Theory of Human Motivation, which he subsequently extended to include his observations of humans' innate curiosity.

Maslow studied what he called exemplary people such as Albert Einstein, Jane Addams, Eleanor Roosevelt, and Frederick Douglass rather than mentally ill or neurotic people, writing that 'the study of crippled, stunted, immature, and unhealthy specimens can yield only a cripple psychology and a cripple philosophy.' Maslow also studied the healthiest one percent of the college student population. In his book, The Farther Reaches of Human Nature, Maslow writes, 'By ordinary standards of this kind of laboratory research...

a. Power III
b. 6-3-5 Brainwriting
c. Hierarchy of needs
d. 180SearchAssistant

13. _________ is a term that has been used in various psychology theories, often in slightly different ways (e.g., Goldstein, Maslow, Rogers.) The term was originally introduced by the organismic theorist Kurt Goldstein for the motive to realise all of one's potentialities. In his view, it is the master motive--indeed, the only real motive a person has, all others being merely manifestations of it.

a. Self-actualization
b. 180SearchAssistant
c. 6-3-5 Brainwriting
d. Power III

14. _________ is a branch of philosophy which seeks to address questions about morality, such as how a moral outcome can be achieved in a specific situation (applied _________), how moral values should be determined (normative _________), what moral values people actually abide by (descriptive _________), what the fundamental semantic, ontological, and epistemic nature of _________ or morality is (meta-_________), and how moral capacity or moral agency develops and what its nature is (moral psychology.)

Socrates was one of the first Greek philosophers to encourage both scholars and the common citizen to turn their attention from the outside world to the condition of man. In this view, Knowledge having a bearing on human life was placed highest, all other knowledge being secondary.

a. ADTECH
b. AMAX
c. Ethics
d. ACNielsen

15. _________ is defined by the American _________ Association as the activity, set of institutions, and processes for creating, communicating, delivering, and exchanging offerings that have value for customers, clients, partners, and society at large. The term developed from the original meaning which referred literally to going to market, as in shopping, or going to a market to sell goods or services.

_________ practice tends to be seen as a creative industry, which includes advertising, distribution and selling.

a. Marketing myopia
b. Customer acquisition management
c. Product naming
d. Marketing

16. _________ is the study of when, why, how, where and what people do or do not buy products. It blends elements from psychology, sociology,social psychology, anthropology and economics. It attempts to understand the buyer decision making process, both individually and in groups. It studies characteristics of individual consumers such as demographics and behavioural variables in an attempt to understand people's wants. It also tries to assess influences on the consumer from groups such as family, friends, reference groups, and society in general.

a. Consumer confidence
b. Multidimensional scaling
c. Communal marketing
d. Consumer behavior

17. _________ involves disseminating information about a product, product line, brand, or company. It is one of the four key aspects of the marketing mix. (The other three elements are product marketing, pricing, and distribution). P>_________ is generally sub-divided into two parts:

- Above the line _________: Promotion in the media (e.g. TV, radio, newspapers, Internet and Mobile Phones) in which the advertiser pays an advertising agency to place the ad
- Below the line _________: All other _________. Much of this is intended to be subtle enough for the consumer to be unaware that _________ is taking place. E.g. sponsorship, product placement, endorsements, sales _________, merchandising, direct mail, personal selling, public relations, trade shows

a. Cashmere Agency
b. Bottling lines
c. Promotion
d. Davie Brown Index

18. _________ was originally coined by Austrian psychologist Alfred Adler in 1929. The current broader sense of the word dates from 1961.

In sociology, a _________ is the way a person lives.

a. 6-3-5 Brainwriting
b. Power III
c. Lifestyle
d. 180SearchAssistant

19. _________ or self identity refers to the global understanding a sentient being has of him or herself. It presupposes but can be distinguished from self-consciousness, which is simply an awareness of one's self. It is also more general than self-esteem, which is the purely evaluative element of the _________.

a. Power III
b. 180SearchAssistant
c. Need for cognition
d. Self-concept

20. A _________ is a sociological concept referring to a group to which an individual or another group is compared.

_________s are used in order to evaluate and determine the nature of a given individual or other group's characteristics and sociological attributes. It is the group to which the individual relates or aspires relate himself or self psychologically.

a. Power III
b. Mociology
c. Minority
d. Reference group

21. _________ is a concept that arose out of the theory of two-step flow of communication propounded by Paul Lazarsfeld and Elihu Katz. This theory is one of several models that try to explain the diffusion of innovations, ideas, or commercial products.

The opinion leader is the agent who is an active media user and who interprets the meaning of media messages or content for lower-end media users.

a. Intellectual property
b. ACNielsen
c. Elasticity
d. Opinion leadership

22. In sociology, anthropology and cultural studies, a _________ is a group of people with a culture (whether distinct or hidden) which differentiates them from the larger culture to which they belong. If a particular _________ is characterized by a systematic opposition to the dominant culture, it may be described as a counterculture. As Ken Gelder notes, _________s are social, with their own shared conventions, values and rituals, but they can also seem 'immersed' or self-absorbed--another feature that distinguishes them from countercultures.

a. Power III
b. 180SearchAssistant
c. 6-3-5 Brainwriting
d. Subculture

1. A _________ is a company or individual that purchases goods or services with the intention of reselling them rather than consuming or using them. This is usually done for profit (but could be resold at a loss.) One example can be found in the industry of telecommunications, where companies buy excess amounts of transmission capacity or call time from other carriers and resell it to smaller carriers.

a. Jobbing house
b. Discontinuation
c. Value-based pricing
d. Reseller

2. A _________ is a type of business entity in which partners (owners) share with each other the profits or losses of the business undertaking in which all have invested. _________s are often favored over corporations for taxation purposes, as the _________ structure does not generally incur a tax on profits before it is distributed to the partners (i.e. there is no dividend tax levied.) However, depending on the _________ structure and the jurisdiction in which it operates, owners of a _________ may be exposed to greater personal liability than they would as shareholders of a corporation.

a. Fair Debt Collection Practices Act
b. Partnership
c. Brand piracy
d. Competition law

3. In statistics, an _________ is a term in a statistical model added when the effect of two or more variables is not simply additive. Such a term reflects that the effect of one variable depends on the values of one or more other variables.

Thus, for a response Y and two variables x_1 and x_2 an additive model would be:

$$Y = ax_1 + bx_2 + \text{error}$$

In contrast to this,

$$Y = ax_1 + bx_2 + c(x_1 \times x_2) + \text{error},$$

is an example of a model with an _________ between variables x_1 and x_2 ('error' refers to the random variable whose value by which y differs from the expected value of y.)

a. AMAX
b. ACNielsen
c. ADTECH
d. Interaction

4. _________ is defined by the American _________ Association as the activity, set of institutions, and processes for creating, communicating, delivering, and exchanging offerings that have value for customers, clients, partners, and society at large. The term developed from the original meaning which referred literally to going to market, as in shopping, or going to a market to sell goods or services.

_________ practice tends to be seen as a creative industry, which includes advertising, distribution and selling.

a. Product naming
b. Marketing
c. Customer acquisition management
d. Marketing myopia

5. _________ is that part of statistical practice concerned with the selection of individual observations intended to yield some knowledge about a population of concern, especially for the purposes of statistical inference. Each observation measures one or more properties (weight, location, etc.) of an observable entity enumerated to distinguish objects or individuals.

a. Richard Buckminster 'Bucky' Fuller
b. Sports Marketing Group
c. AStore
d. Sampling

6. In economics, _________ is the desire to own something and the ability to pay for it. The term _________ signifies the ability or the willingness to buy a particular commodity at a given point of time .

.

a. Market dominance
b. Market system
c. Demand
d. Discretionary spending

7. _________ is a term in economics, where demand for one good or service occurs as a result of demand for another. This may occur as the former is a part of production of the second. For example, demand for coal leads to _________ for mining, as coal must be mined for coal to be consumed.

a. 6-3-5 Brainwriting
b. 180SearchAssistant
c. Power III
d. Derived demand

8. In economics, _________ describes demand that is not very sensitive to a change in price.

a. ACNielsen
b. ADTECH
c. Inelastic
d. AMAX

9. A _________, in marketing, procurement, and organizational studies, is a group of employees, family members, or members of any type of organization responsible for purchasing an item for the organization. In a business setting, major purchases typically require input from various parts of the organization, including finance, accounting, purchasing, information technology management, and senior management. Highly technical purchases, such as information systems or production equipment, also require the expertise of technical specialists.

a. Commercialization
b. Packshot
c. Marketing myopia
d. Buying center

10. _________ is a broad label that refers to any individuals or households that use goods and services generated within the economy. The concept of a _________ is used in different contexts, so that the usage and significance of the term may vary.

A _________ is a person who uses any product or service.

a. 6-3-5 Brainwriting
b. Power III
c. Consumer
d. 180SearchAssistant

11. A personal and cultural _________ is a relative ethic _________, an assumption upon which implementation can be extrapolated. A _________ system is a set of consistent _________s and measures that is soo not true. A principle _________ is a foundation upon which other _________s and measures of integrity are based.

a. Perceptual maps
b. Value
c. Supreme Court of the United States
d. Package-on-Package

12.

_________ is a systematic method to improve the 'value' of goods or products and services by using an examination of function. Value, as defined, is the ratio of function to cost. Value can therefore be increased by either improving the function or reducing the cost.

a. Power III
b. 180SearchAssistant
c. Productivity
d. Value engineering

13. The Oxford University Press defines _________ as 'marketing on a worldwide scale reconciling or taking commercial advantage of global operational differences, similarities and opportunities in order to meet global objectives.' Oxford University Press' Glossary of Marketing Terms.

Here are three reasons for the shift from domestic to _________ as given by the authors of the textbook, _________ Management--3rd Edition by Masaaki Kotabe and Kristiaan Helsen, 2004.

One of the product categories in which global competition has been easy to track is in U.S. automotive sales.

a. Guerrilla Marketing
b. Diversity marketing
c. Digital marketing
d. Global marketing

14. On an intranet or B2E Enterprise Web portals, personalization is often based on user attributes such as department, functional area, or role. The term _________ in this context refers to the ability of users to modify the page layout or specify what content should be displayed.

There are two categories of personalizations:

1. Rule-based
2. Content-based

Web personalization models include rules-based filtering, based on 'if this, then that' rules processing, and collaborative filtering, which serves relevant material to customers by combining their own personal preferences with the preferences of like-minded others. Collaborative filtering works well for books, music, video, etc.

a. Self branding
b. Cashmere Agency
c. Movin'
d. Customization

15. _________ in its literal sense is the process of transformation of local or regional phenomena into global ones. It can be described as a process by which the people of the world are unified into a single society and function together.

This process is a combination of economic, technological, sociocultural and political forces.

a. Globalization
b. 6-3-5 Brainwriting
c. 180SearchAssistant
d. Power III

16. A _________ is a process that can allow an organization to concentrate its limited resources on the greatest opportunities to increase sales and achieve a sustainable competitive advantage. A _________ should be centered around the key concept that customer satisfaction is the main goal.

A _________ is most effective when it is an integral component of corporate strategy, defining how the organization will successfully engage customers, prospects, and competitors in the market arena.

a. Psychographic
b. Marketing strategy
c. Cyberdoc
d. Societal marketing

17. _________, also referred to as i-marketing, web marketing, online marketing is the marketing of products or services over the Internet.

The Internet has brought many unique benefits to marketing, one of which being lower costs for the distribution of information and media to a global audience. The interactive nature of _________, both in terms of providing instant response and eliciting responses, is a unique quality of the medium.

a. ADTECH
b. ACNielsen
c. AMAX
d. Internet marketing

18. An _________ is the manufacturing of a good or service within a category. Although _________ is a broad term for any kind of economic production, in economics and urban planning _________ is a synonym for the secondary sector, which is a type of economic activity involved in the manufacturing of raw materials into goods and products.

There are four key industrial economic sectors: the primary sector, largely raw material extraction industries such as mining and farming; the secondary sector, involving refining, construction, and manufacturing; the tertiary sector, which deals with services (such as law and medicine) and distribution of manufactured goods; and the quaternary sector, a relatively new type of knowledge _________ focusing on technological research, design and development such as computer programming, and biochemistry.

a. ACNielsen
b. Industry
c. AMAX
d. ADTECH

19. The _________ or _________ is used by business and government to classify and measure economic activity in Canada, Mexico and the United States. It has largely replaced the older Standard Industrial Classification system; however, certain government departments and agencies, such as the U.S. Securities and Exchange Commission (SEC), still use the SIC codes.

The _________ numbering system is a six-digit code.

a. 6-3-5 Brainwriting
b. 180SearchAssistant
c. Power III
d. North American Industry Classification System

20. _________ refer to a collection of facts usually collected as the result of experience, observation or experiment or a set of premises. This may consist of numbers, words particularly as measurements or observations of a set of variables. _________ are often viewed as a lowest level of abstraction from which information and knowledge are derived.

a. Sample size
b. Mean
c. Pearson product-moment correlation coefficient
d. Data

1. _________ is an advertisement in which a particular product specifically mentions a competitor by name for the express purpose of showing why the competitor is inferior to the product naming it.

This should not be confused with parody advertisements, where a fictional product is being advertised for the purpose of poking fun at the particular advertisement, nor should it be confused with the use of a coined brand name for the purpose of comparing the product without actually naming an actual competitor. ('Wikipedia tastes better and is less filling than the Encyclopedia Galactica.')

In the 1980s, during what has been referred to as the cola wars, soft-drink manufacturer Pepsi ran a series of advertisements where people, caught on hidden camera, in a blind taste test, chose Pepsi over rival Coca-Cola.

a. Heavy-up
b. Comparative advertising
c. Cost per conversion
d. GL-70

2. _________ is a broad label that refers to any individuals or households that use goods and services generated within the economy. The concept of a _________ is used in different contexts, so that the usage and significance of the term may vary.

A _________ is a person who uses any product or service.

a. 180SearchAssistant
b. Consumer
c. Power III
d. 6-3-5 Brainwriting

3. _________ is anything that is intended to save time, energy or frustration. A _________ store at a petrol station, for example, sells items that have nothing to do with gasoline/petrol, but it saves the consumer from having to go to a grocery store. '_________' is a very relative term and its meaning tends to change over time.

a. MaxDiff
b. Demographic profile
c. Convenience
d. Marketing buzz

4. _________ is the examining of goods or services from retailers with the intent to purchase at that time. _________ is an activity of selection and/or purchase. In some contexts it is considered a leisure activity as well as an economic one.

a. Khodebshchik
b. Discount store
c. Hawkers
d. Shopping

5. A _________ is something that is acted upon or used by or by human labour or industry, for use as a building material to create some product or structure. Often the term is used to denote material that came from nature and is in an unprocessed or minimally processed state. Iron ore, logs, and crude oil, would be examples.

a. 6-3-5 Brainwriting
b. Power III
c. 180SearchAssistant
d. Raw material

6. There are many important decisions about product and service development and marketing. In the process of product development and marketing we should focus on strategic decisions about product attributes, product branding, product packaging, product labeling and product support services. But product strategy also calls for building a _________.

a. Product line
b. Technology acceptance model
c. Pinstorm
d. Macromarketing

7. A _________ dominated business thought from the beginning of capitalism to the mid 1950s, and some argue it still exists in some industries. Business concerned itself primarily with production, manufacturing, and efficiency issues. Say's Law encapsulated this viewpoint, stating: 'Supply creates its own demand'.

a. Production orientation
b. Product differentiation
c. Marketing
d. Blitz QFD

8. _________ Management is the succession of strategies used by management as a product goes through its _________. The conditions in which a product is sold changes over time and must be managed as it moves through its succession of stages.

The _________ goes through many phases, involves many professional disciplines, and requires many skills, tools and processes.

a. Customer satisfaction
b. Chain stores
c. Supplier diversity
d. Product life cycle

9. A _________ is a collection of symbols, experiences and associations connected with a product, a service, a person or any other artifact or entity.

_________s have become increasingly important components of culture and the economy, now being described as 'cultural accessories and personal philosophies'.

Some people distinguish the psychological aspect of a _________ from the experiential aspect.

a. Brand
b. Brand equity
c. Store brand
d. Brandable software

10. _________ in economics and business is the result of an exchange and from that trade we assign a numerical monetary value to a good, service or asset. If I trade 4 apples for an orange, the _________ of an orange is 4 - apples. Inversely, the _________ of an apple is 1/4 oranges.

a. Discounts and allowances
b. Pricing
c. Contribution margin-based pricing
d. Price

11. _________ is defined by the American _________ Association as the activity, set of institutions, and processes for creating, communicating, delivering, and exchanging offerings that have value for customers, clients, partners, and society at large. The term developed from the original meaning which referred literally to going to market, as in shopping, or going to a market to sell goods or services.

_________ practice tends to be seen as a creative industry, which includes advertising, distribution and selling.

a. Marketing myopia
b. Customer acquisition management
c. Product naming
d. Marketing

1. A product _________ is the use of an established product's brand name for a new item in the same product category._________s occur when a company introduces additional items in the same product category under the same brand name such as new flavors, forms, colors, added ingredients, package sizes.Examples includei) Zen LXI, Zen VXIii) Surf, Surf Excel, Surf Excel Blueiii) Splendour, Splendour Plusiv) Coke, Diet Coke, Vanilla Cokev) Clinic All Clear, Clinic Plus

- brand
- brand management
- marketing
- product management
- Product lining

.

a. Targeted advertising
b. Brand Development Index
c. Perishability
d. Line extension

2. A _________ is the use of an established product's brand name for a new item in the same product category. _________s occur when a company introduces additional items in the same product category under the same brand name such as new flavors, forms, colors, added ingredients, package sizes.

a. Pearson's chi-square
b. Retail floor planning
c. Comparison-Shopping agent
d. Product line extension

3. There are many important decisions about product and service development and marketing. In the process of product development and marketing we should focus on strategic decisions about product attributes, product branding, product packaging, product labeling and product support services. But product strategy also calls for building a _________.

a. Technology acceptance model
b. Product line
c. Pinstorm
d. Macromarketing

4. _________ in economics and business is the result of an exchange and from that trade we assign a numerical monetary value to a good, service or asset. If I trade 4 apples for an orange, the _________ of an orange is 4 - apples. Inversely, the _________ of an apple is 1/4 oranges.

a. Discounts and allowances
b. Pricing
c. Price
d. Contribution margin-based pricing

5. _________ is the process of using quantitative methods and qualitative methods to evaluate consumer response to a product idea prior to the introduction of a product to the market. It can also be used to generate communication designed to alter consumer attitudes toward existing products. These methods involve the evaluation by consumers of product concepts having certain rational benefits, such as 'a detergent that removes stains but is gentle on fabrics,' or non-rational benefits, such as 'a shampoo that lets you be yourself.' Such methods are commonly referred to as _________ and have been performed using field surveys, personal interviews and focus groups, in combination with various quantitative methods, to generate and evaluate product concepts.

a. Cross tabulation
b. Logit analysis
c. Concept testing
d. Market analysis

6. In business and engineering, _________ is the term used to describe the complete process of bringing a new product or service to market. There are two parallel paths involved in the _________ process: one involves the idea generation, product design, and detail engineering; the other involves market research and marketing analysis. Companies typically see _________ as the first stage in generating and commercializing new products within the overall strategic process of product life cycle management used to maintain or grow their market share.

a. Specification
b. Product optimization
c. Product development
d. New product development

7. In business and engineering, new _________ is the term used to describe the complete process of bringing a new product or service to market. There are two parallel paths involved in the Nproduct development process: one involves the idea generation, product design, and detail engineering; the other involves market research and marketing analysis. Companies typically see new _________ as the first stage in generating and commercializing new products within the overall strategic process of product life cycle management used to maintain or grow their market share.

a. New product screening
b. New product development
c. Product development
d. Specification tree

8. _________ is the set of tasks, knowledge, and techniques required to identify business needs and determine solutions to business problems. Solutions often include a systems development component, but may also consist of process improvement or organizational change. The person who carries out this task is called a business analyst or _________.

a. Door-to-door
b. Marketing management
c. Fast moving consumer goods
d. Business analysis

9. A _________, in the field of business and marketing, is a geographic region or demographic group used to gauge the viability of a product or service in the mass market prior to a wide scale roll-out. The criteria used to judge the acceptability of a _________ region or group include:

1. a population that is demographically similar to the proposed target market; and
2. relative isolation from densely populated media markets so that advertising to the test audience can be efficient and economical.

The _________ ideally aims to duplicate 'everything' - promotion and distribution as well as `product' - on a smaller scale. The technique replicates, typically in one area, what is planned to occur in a national launch; and the results are very carefully monitored, so that they can be extrapolated to projected national results. The `area' may be any one of the following:

- Television area
- Test town
- Residential neighborhood
- Test site

A number of decisions have to be taken about any _________:

- Which _________?
- What is to be tested?
- How long a test?
- What are the success criteria?

The simple go or no-go decision, together with the related reduction of risk, is normally the main justification for the expense of _________s. At the same time, however, such _________s can be used to test specific elements of a new product's marketing mix; possibly the version of the product itself, the promotional message and media spend, the distribution channels and the price.

a. Power III
b. Test market
c. 180SearchAssistant
d. Preadolescence

10. _________ is defined by the American _________ Association as the activity, set of institutions, and processes for creating, communicating, delivering, and exchanging offerings that have value for customers, clients, partners, and society at large. The term developed from the original meaning which referred literally to going to market, as in shopping, or going to a market to sell goods or services.

_________ practice tends to be seen as a creative industry, which includes advertising, distribution and selling.

a. Product naming
b. Marketing myopia
c. Customer acquisition management
d. Marketing

11. _________ is the process or cycle of introducing a new product into the market. The actual launch of a new product is the final stage of new product development, and the one where the most money will have to be spent for advertising, sales promotion, and other marketing efforts. In the case of a new consumer packaged good, costs will be at least $ 10 million, but can reach up to $ 200 million.

a. Commercialization
b. Customer Interaction Tracker
c. Confusion marketing
d. Sweepstakes

12. In marketing, _________ is the process of distinguishing the differences of a product or offering from others, to make it more attractive to a particular target market. This involves differentiating it from competitors' products as well as one's own product offerings.

Differentiation is a source of competitive advantage.

a. Packshot
b. Marketing myopia
c. Product differentiation
d. Corporate image

13. _________ is one of the four Ps of the marketing mix. The other three aspects are product, promotion, and place. It is also a key variable in microeconomic price allocation theory.

a. Price
b. Competitor indexing
c. Pricing
d. Relationship based pricing

14. _________ is the provision of service to customers before, during and after a purchase.

According to Turban et al., '_________ is a series of activities designed to enhance the level of customer satisfaction - that is, the feeling that a product or service has met the customer expectation.'

Its importance varies by product, industry and customer.

a. COPC Inc.
b. Facing
c. Customer experience
d. Customer service

15. _________ can be defined as the idea generation, concept development, testing and manufacturing or implementation of a physical object or service. _________ers conceptualize and evaluate ideas, making them tangible through products in a more systematic approach. The role of a _________er encompasses many characteristics of the marketing manager, product manager, industrial designer and design engineer.

a. Product design
b. AStore
c. Albert Einstein
d. African Americans

16. _________ is a service provided by many retailers of various products, primarily electronics, that provides the end-user with a resource for information regarding the product, and help if the product should malfunction. _________ can be found in most manuals for products in the form of a phone number, website address, or physical location.

The Internet has allowed for a new form of _________ to develop.

a. Psychological pricing
b. Product support
c. Product life cycle
d. Price-weighted

17. _________ is an advertisement in which a particular product specifically mentions a competitor by name for the express purpose of showing why the competitor is inferior to the product naming it.

This should not be confused with parody advertisements, where a fictional product is being advertised for the purpose of poking fun at the particular advertisement, nor should it be confused with the use of a coined brand name for the purpose of comparing the product without actually naming an actual competitor. ('Wikipedia tastes better and is less filling than the Encyclopedia Galactica.')

In the 1980s, during what has been referred to as the cola wars, soft-drink manufacturer Pepsi ran a series of advertisements where people, caught on hidden camera, in a blind taste test, chose Pepsi over rival Coca-Cola.

a. Cost per conversion
b. Comparative advertising
c. Heavy-up
d. GL-70

18. In marketing, _________ has come to mean the process by which marketers try to create an image or identity in the minds of their target market for its product, brand, or organization. It is the 'relative competitive comparison' their product occupies in a given market as perceived by the target market.

Re-_________ involves changing the identity of a product, relative to the identity of competing products, in the collective minds of the target market.

a. Containerization
b. Moratorium
c. GE matrix
d. Positioning

19. A _________ is a collection of symbols, experiences and associations connected with a product, a service, a person or any other artifact or entity.

_________s have become increasingly important components of culture and the economy, now being described as 'cultural accessories and personal philosophies'.

Some people distinguish the psychological aspect of a _________ from the experiential aspect.

a. Brand
b. Store brand
c. Brand equity
d. Brandable software

20. A _________ researches, selects, develops, and places a company's products.

A _________ considers numerous factors such as target demographic, the products offered by the competition, and how well the product fits in with the company's business model. Generally, a _________ manages one or more tangible products.

a. Power III
b. Product manager
c. Pick and pack
d. Promotional mix

1. A _________ is a collection of symbols, experiences and associations connected with a product, a service, a person or any other artifact or entity.

_________s have become increasingly important components of culture and the economy, now being described as 'cultural accessories and personal philosophies'.

Some people distinguish the psychological aspect of a _________ from the experiential aspect.

a. Store brand
b. Brand equity
c. Brand
d. Brandable software

2. A _________ is the name which a business trades under for commercial purposes, although its registered, legal name, used for contracts and other formal situations, may be another. Pharmaceuticals also have _________s, often dissimilar to their chemical names

Trading names are sometimes registered as trademarks or are regarded as brands.

a. Local purchasing
b. Niche market
c. Soft currency
d. Trade name

3. A _________ or trade mark, identified by the symbols â„¢ (not yet registered) and Â® (registered) business organization or other legal entity to identify that the products and/or services to consumers with which the _________ appears originate from a unique source of origin, and to distinguish its products or services from those of other entities. A _________ is a type of intellectual property, and typically a name, word, phrase, logo, symbol, design, image, or a combination of these elements. There is also a range of non-conventional _________s comprising marks which do not fall into these standard categories.

a. 180SearchAssistant
b. Risk management
c. Power III
d. Trademark

4. A personal and cultural _________ is a relative ethic _________, an assumption upon which implementation can be extrapolated. A _________ system is a set of consistent _________s and measures that is soo not true. A principle _________ is a foundation upon which other _________s and measures of integrity are based.

a. Supreme Court of the United States
b. Perceptual maps
c. Package-on-Package
d. Value

5. _________, in marketing, consists of a consumer's commitment to repurchase the brand and can be demonstrated by repeated buying of a product or service or other positive behaviors such as word of mouth advocacy. True _________ implies that the consumer is willing, at least on occasion, to put aside their own desires in the interest of the brand. _________ has been proclaimed by some to be the ultimate goal of marketing.

a. Brand implementation
b. Brand awareness
c. Trade Symbols
d. Brand loyalty

6. A brand which is widely known in the marketplace acquires _________. When _________ builds up to a point where a brand enjoys a critical mass of positive sentiment in the marketplace, it is said to have achieved brand franchise. One goal in _________ is the identification of a brand without the name of the company present.

a. Trade Symbols
b. Brand blunder
c. Trademark distinctiveness
d. Brand recognition

7. _________ refers to the marketing effects or outcomes that accrue to a product with its brand name compared with those that would accrue if the same product did not have the brand name . And, at the root of these marketing effects is consumers' knowledge. In other words, consumers' knowledge about a brand makes manufacturers/advertisers respond differently or adopt appropriately adapt measures for the marketing of the brand .

a. Brand aversion
b. Brand image
c. Product extension
d. Brand equity

8. _________ is when a large distribution channel member (usually a retailer), buys from a manufacturer in bulk and puts its own name on the product. This strategy is only practical when the retailer does very high levels of volume. The advantages to the retailer are:

- more freedom and flexibility in pricing
- more control over product attributes and quality
- higher margins (or lower selling price)
- eliminates much of the manufacturer's promotional costs

The advantages to the manufacturer are:

- reduced promotional costs
- stability of sales volume (at least while the contract is operative)

- Kumar, Nirmalya; Steenkamp, Jan-Benedict E.M., Private Label Strategy - How to Meet the Store Brand Challenge. Harvard Business Press 2007

- private label
- brand management
- brand
- product management
- marketing

.

a. Private branding
b. Promotion
c. Customization
d. Rural market

9. _________s (house brands in the United States, own brands in the UK, and home brands in Australia) are brands which are specific to a retail store or store chain. The retailer can manufacture goods under its own label, re-brand private label goods, or outsource manufacture of _________ items to multiple third parties - often the same manufacturers that produce brand label goods. _________ goods are generally cheaper than national brand goods because the retailer can optimize the production to suit consumer demand and reduce advertising costs.

a. Brand strength analysis
b. Brand ambassador
c. Store brand
d. Brand loyalty

10. _________ is one of the four elements of marketing mix. An organization or set of organizations (go-betweens) involved in the process of making a product or service available for use or consumption by a consumer or business user.

The other three parts of the marketing mix are product, pricing, and promotion.

a. Comparison-Shopping agent
b. Distribution
c. Better Living Through Chemistry
d. Japan Advertising Photographers' Association

11. _________ of consumer products (often supermarket goods) are distinguished by the absence of a brand name.They are identifed more by product characterstics.

They may be manufactured by less [prominent companies], or manufactured on the same production line as a 'named' brand. _________ are usually priced below those products sold by supermarkets under their own brand (frequently referred to as 'store brands' or 'own brands'.)

a. M80
b. Gross Margin Return on Inventory Investment
c. Micro ads
d. Generic brands

12. _________ in economics and business is the result of an exchange and from that trade we assign a numerical monetary value to a good, service or asset. If I trade 4 apples for an orange, the _________ of an orange is 4 - apples. Inversely, the _________ of an apple is 1/4 oranges.

a. Price
b. Contribution margin-based pricing
c. Discounts and allowances
d. Pricing

13. _________ is the marketing strategy of giving each product in a product portfolio its own unique brand name. This is contrasted with family branding in which the products in a product line are given the same brand name. The advantage of _________ is that each product has a self image and identity that's unique.

a. Intangibility
b. Individual branding
c. Online focus group
d. Engagement

14. _________ is a marketing strategy that involves selling several related products under one brand name. It is contrasted with individual branding in which each product in a portfolio is given a unique identity and brand name.

There are often economies of scope associated with _________ since several products can efficiently be promoted with a single advertisement or campaign.

a. 180SearchAssistant
b. 6-3-5 Brainwriting
c. Power III
d. Family branding

15. _________ refers to several different marketing arrangements:

_________ is when two companies form an alliance to work together, creating marketing synergy. As described in _________: The Science of Alliance:

_________ is an arrangement that associates a single product or service with more than one brand name, or otherwise associates a product with someone other than the principal producer. The typical _________ agreement involves two or more companies acting in cooperation to associate any of various logos, color schemes, or brand identifiers to a specific product that is contractually designated for this purpose.

a. Co-branding
b. Line extension
c. Target audience
d. Brand Development Index

16. _________ is the process of creating and managing contracts between the owner of a brand and a company or individual who wants to use the brand in association with a product, for an agreed period of time, within an agreed territory. Licensing is used by brand owners to extend a trademark or character onto products of a completely different nature.

_________ a is well-established business, both in the area of patents and trademarks.

a. Brand culture
b. Brand strength analysis
c. Brand loyalty
d. Brand licensing

17. The verb _________ or grant _________ means to give permission. The noun _________ refers to that permission as well as to the document memorializing that permission. _________ may be granted by a party to another party as an element of an agreement between those parties.

a. Power III
b. 180SearchAssistant
c. License
d. 6-3-5 Brainwriting

18. A _________ is a list of the general tasks and responsibilities of a position. Typically, it also includes to whom the position reports, specifications such as the qualifications needed by the person in the job, salary range for the position, etc. A _________ is usually developed by conducting a job analysis, which includes examining the tasks and sequences of tasks necessary to perform the job.

a. 6-3-5 Brainwriting
b. Power III
c. 180SearchAssistant
d. Job description

19. _________ is defined by the American _________ Association as the activity, set of institutions, and processes for creating, communicating, delivering, and exchanging offerings that have value for customers, clients, partners, and society at large. The term developed from the original meaning which referred literally to going to market, as in shopping, or going to a market to sell goods or services.

_________ practice tends to be seen as a creative industry, which includes advertising, distribution and selling.

a. Marketing
b. Customer acquisition management
c. Product naming
d. Marketing myopia

20. A _________ is a process that can allow an organization to concentrate its limited resources on the greatest opportunities to increase sales and achieve a sustainable competitive advantage. A _________ should be centered around the key concept that customer satisfaction is the main goal.

A _________ is most effective when it is an integral component of corporate strategy, defining how the organization will successfully engage customers, prospects, and competitors in the market arena.

a. Psychographic
b. Cyberdoc
c. Marketing strategy
d. Societal marketing

21. A _________ is a plan of action designed to achieve a particular goal.

_________ is different from tactics. In military terms, tactics is concerned with the conduct of an engagement while _________ is concerned with how different engagements are linked.

a. Power III
b. Strategy
c. 6-3-5 Brainwriting
d. 180SearchAssistant

22. The _________ is a US law that applies to labels on many consumer products. It requires the label to state:

- The identity of the product;
- The name and place of business of the manufacturer, packer, or distributor; and
- The net quantity of contents.

The contents statement must include both metric and U.S. customary units.

Passed under Lyndon B. Johnson in 1966, the law first took effect on July 1, 1967. The metric labeling requirement was added in 1992 and took effect on February 14, 1994.

a. 6-3-5 Brainwriting
b. 180SearchAssistant
c. Power III
d. Fair Packaging and Labeling Act

23. The U.S. _________ is an agency of the United States Department of Health and Human Services and is responsible for regulating and supervising the safety of foods, dietary supplements, drugs, vaccines, biological medical products, blood products, medical devices, radiation-emitting devices, veterinary products, and cosmetics. The FDA also enforces section 361 of the Public Health Service Act and the associated regulations, including sanitation requirements on interstate travel as well as specific rules for control of disease on products ranging from pet turtles to semen donations for assisted reproductive medicine techniques.

The FDA is an agency within the United States Department of Health and Human Services responsible for protecting and promoting the nation's public health.

a. Power III
b. 6-3-5 Brainwriting
c. 180SearchAssistant
d. Food and Drug Administration

24. The _________ is a 1990 United States Federal law. It was signed into law on November 8, 1990 by the president.

The law gives the Food and Drug Administration (FDA) authority to require nutrition labeling of most foods regulated by the Agency; and to require that all nutrient content claims (for example, 'high fiber', 'low fat', etc).

a. Nutrition Labeling and Education Act
b. Copyright infringement
c. Fair Debt Collection Practices Act
d. Trespass to land

25. The _________ is an independent agency of the United States government, established in 1914 by the _________ Act. Its principal mission is the promotion of 'consumer protection' and the elimination and prevention of what regulators perceive to be harmfully 'anti-competitive' business practices, such as coercive monopoly.

The _________ Act was one of President Wilson's major acts against trusts.

a. Power III
b. Federal Trade Commission
c. 6-3-5 Brainwriting
d. 180SearchAssistant

1. _________ is an advertisement in which a particular product specifically mentions a competitor by name for the express purpose of showing why the competitor is inferior to the product naming it.

This should not be confused with parody advertisements, where a fictional product is being advertised for the purpose of poking fun at the particular advertisement, nor should it be confused with the use of a coined brand name for the purpose of comparing the product without actually naming an actual competitor. ('Wikipedia tastes better and is less filling than the Encyclopedia Galactica.')

In the 1980s, during what has been referred to as the cola wars, soft-drink manufacturer Pepsi ran a series of advertisements where people, caught on hidden camera, in a blind taste test, chose Pepsi over rival Coca-Cola.

a. Cost per conversion
b. GL-70
c. Comparative advertising
d. Heavy-up

2. _________ is used in marketing to describe the inability to assess the value gained from engaging in an activity using any tangible evidence. It is often used to describe services where there isn't a tangible product that the customer can purchase, that can be seen, tasted or touched.

Other key characteristics of services include perishability, inseparability and variability.

a. Automated surveys
b. Individual branding
c. Inseparability
d. Intangibility

3. _________ is used in marketing to describe a key quality of services as distinct from goods. _________ is the characteristic that a service has which renders it impossible to divorce the supply or production of the service from its consumption.

Other key characteristics of services include perishability, intangibility and variability.

a. Individual branding
b. Online focus group
c. Inseparability
d. Engagement

4. _________ is used in marketing to describe the way in which service capacity cannot be stored for sale in the future. It is a key concept of services marketing.

Other key characteristics of services include intangibility, inseparability and variability.

a. Specialty catalogs
b. National brand
c. Perishability
d. Demonstrator model

5. _________ involves disseminating information about a product, product line, brand, or company. It is one of the four key aspects of the marketing mix. (The other three elements are product marketing, pricing, and distribution). P>_________ is generally sub-divided into two parts:

- Above the line _________: Promotion in the media (e.g. TV, radio, newspapers, Internet and Mobile Phones) in which the advertiser pays an advertising agency to place the ad
- Below the line _________: All other _________. Much of this is intended to be subtle enough for the consumer to be unaware that _________ is taking place. E.g. sponsorship, product placement, endorsements, sales _________, merchandising, direct mail, personal selling, public relations, trade shows

a. Bottling lines
b. Davie Brown Index
c. Cashmere Agency
d. Promotion

6. _________ is defined by the American _________ Association as the activity, set of institutions, and processes for creating, communicating, delivering, and exchanging offerings that have value for customers, clients, partners, and society at large. The term developed from the original meaning which referred literally to going to market, as in shopping, or going to a market to sell goods or services.

_________ practice tends to be seen as a creative industry, which includes advertising, distribution and selling.

a. Product naming
b. Customer acquisition management
c. Marketing myopia
d. Marketing

7. The _________ is generally accepted as the use and specification of the four p's describing the strategic position of a product in the marketplace. One version of the origins of the _________ starts in 1948 when James Culliton said that a marketing decision should be a result of something similar to a recipe. This version continued in 1953 when Neil Borden, in his American Marketing Association presidential address, took the recipe idea one step further and coined the term 'Marketing-Mix'.

a. 6-3-5 Brainwriting
b. Power III
c. 180SearchAssistant
d. Marketing mix

8. _________ is marketing based on relationship and value. It may be used to market a service or a product.

Marketing a service-base business is different from marketing a goods-base business.

a. Services Marketing
b. 180SearchAssistant
c. Power III
d. 6-3-5 Brainwriting

9. _________ is one of the four elements of marketing mix. An organization or set of organizations (go-betweens) involved in the process of making a product or service available for use or consumption by a consumer or business user.

The other three parts of the marketing mix are product, pricing, and promotion.

a. Better Living Through Chemistry
b. Japan Advertising Photographers' Association
c. Comparison-Shopping agent
d. Distribution

10. _________ or personalisation is tailoring a consumer product, electronic or written medium to a user based on personal details or characteristics they provide. More recently, it has especially been applied in the context of the World Wide Web.

Web pages are personalized based on the interests of an individual.

a. Complex sale
b. Personalization
c. Sexism,
d. Flighting

11. _________ in economics and business is the result of an exchange and from that trade we assign a numerical monetary value to a good, service or asset. If I trade 4 apples for an orange, the _________ of an orange is 4 - apples. Inversely, the _________ of an apple is 1/4 oranges.

a. Pricing
b. Discounts and allowances
c. Contribution margin-based pricing
d. Price

12. _________ is one of the four Ps of the marketing mix. The other three aspects are product, promotion, and place. It is also a key variable in microeconomic price allocation theory.

a. Competitor indexing
b. Pricing
c. Price
d. Relationship based pricing

13. _________ is systematic determination of merit, worth, and significance of something or someone using criteria against a set of standards. _________ often is used to characterize and appraise subjects of interest in a wide range of human enterprises, including the arts, criminal justice, foundations and non-profit organizations, government, health care, and other human services.

Depending on the topic of interest, there are professional groups which look to the quality and rigor of the _________ process.

a. AMAX
b. Evaluation
c. ACNielsen
d. ADTECH

14. _________ is a form of communication that typically attempts to persuade potential customers to purchase or to consume more of a particular brand of product or service. 'While now central to the contemporary global economy and the reproduction of global production networks, it is only quite recently that _________ has been more than a marginal influence on patterns of sales and production. The formation of modern _________ was intimately bound up with the emergence of new forms of monopoly capitalism around the end of the 19th and beginning of the 20th century as one element in corporate strategies to create, organize and where possible control markets, especially for mass produced consumer goods.

a. AMAX
b. ADTECH
c. ACNielsen
d. Advertising

15. _________ is a contract between two parties, one being the employer and the other being the employee. An employee may be defined as: 'A person in the service of another under any contract of hire, express or implied, oral or written, where the employer has the power or right to control and direct the employee in the material details of how the work is to be performed.' Black's Law Dictionary page 471 (5th ed. 1979.)

a. ADTECH
b. Employment
c. AMAX
d. ACNielsen

16. A _________ is an explicit set of requirements to be satisfied by a material, product, or service.

In engineering, manufacturing, and business, it is vital for suppliers, purchasers, and users of materials, products, or services to understand and agree upon all requirements. A _________ is a type of a standard which is often referenced by a contract or procurement document.

a. Specification
b. Product development
c. Product optimization
d. New product development

17. A _________ is a process that can allow an organization to concentrate its limited resources on the greatest opportunities to increase sales and achieve a sustainable competitive advantage. A _________ should be centered around the key concept that customer satisfaction is the main goal.

A _________ is most effective when it is an integral component of corporate strategy, defining how the organization will successfully engage customers, prospects, and competitors in the market arena.

a. Cyberdoc
b. Societal marketing
c. Psychographic
d. Marketing strategy

18. _________ is a business term meaning the market segment to which a particular good or service is marketed. It is mainly defined by age, gender, geography, socio-economic grouping, technographic, or any other combination of demographics. It is generally studied and mapped by an organization through lists and reports containing demographic information that may have an effect on the marketing of key products or services.

a. Brando
b. Category Development Index
c. Distribution
d. Market specialization

19. _________ or economic opportunity loss is the value of the next best alternative forgone as the result of making a decision. _________ analysis is an important part of a company's decision-making processes but is not treated as an actual cost in any financial statement. The next best thing that a person can engage in is referred to as the _________ of doing the best thing and ignoring the next best thing to be done.

a. Opportunity cost
b. AMAX
c. ACNielsen
d. ADTECH

20. In economics, business, retail, and accounting, a _________ is the value of money that has been used up to produce something, and hence is not available for use anymore. In economics, a _________ is an alternative that is given up as a result of a decision. In business, the _________ may be one of acquisition, in which case the amount of money expended to acquire it is counted as _________.

a. Cost
b. Transaction cost
c. Variable cost
d. Fixed costs

1. _________ is defined by the American _________ Association as the activity, set of institutions, and processes for creating, communicating, delivering, and exchanging offerings that have value for customers, clients, partners, and society at large. The term developed from the original meaning which referred literally to going to market, as in shopping, or going to a market to sell goods or services.

_________ practice tends to be seen as a creative industry, which includes advertising, distribution and selling.

a. Marketing
b. Product naming
c. Customer acquisition management
d. Marketing myopia

2. In economics, _________ is a measure of the relative satisfaction from consumption of various goods and services. Given this measure, one may speak meaningfully of increasing or decreasing _________, and thereby explain economic behavior in terms of attempts to increase one's _________. For illustrative purposes, changes in _________ are sometimes expressed in units called utils.

a. AMAX
b. ACNielsen
c. Utility
d. ADTECH

3. A _________ or logistics network is the system of organizations, people, technology, activities, information and resources involved in moving a product or service from supplier to customer. _________ activities transform natural resources, raw materials and components into a finished product that is delivered to the end customer. In sophisticated _________ systems, used products may re-enter the _________ at any point where residual value is recyclable.

a. Purchasing
b. Supply chain
c. Demand chain management
d. Supply chain network

4. _________ in economics and business is the result of an exchange and from that trade we assign a numerical monetary value to a good, service or asset. If I trade 4 apples for an orange, the _________ of an orange is 4 - apples. Inversely, the _________ of an apple is 1/4 oranges.

a. Discounts and allowances
b. Contribution margin-based pricing
c. Price
d. Pricing

5. _________ is a broad label that refers to any individuals or households that use goods and services generated within the economy. The concept of a _________ is used in different contexts, so that the usage and significance of the term may vary.

A _________ is a person who uses any product or service.

a. 6-3-5 Brainwriting
b. 180SearchAssistant
c. Power III
d. Consumer

6. _________ is one of the four elements of marketing mix. An organization or set of organizations (go-betweens) involved in the process of making a product or service available for use or consumption by a consumer or business user.

The other three parts of the marketing mix are product, pricing, and promotion.

a. Japan Advertising Photographers' Association
b. Comparison-Shopping agent
c. Distribution
d. Better Living Through Chemistry

7. _________ is a business term meaning the market segment to which a particular good or service is marketed. It is mainly defined by age, gender, geography, socio-economic grouping, technographic, or any other combination of demographics. It is generally studied and mapped by an organization through lists and reports containing demographic information that may have an effect on the marketing of key products or services.

a. Distribution | b. Category Development Index
c. Brando | d. Market specialization

8. _________ occurs when manufacturers (brands) disintermediate their channel partners, such as distributors, retailers, dealers, and sales representatives, by selling their products direct to consumers through general marketing methods and/or over the internet through eCommerce.

Some manufacturers want their brands to capture the power of the internet but do not want to create conflict with their other distribution channels, as these partners are necessary and viable for any manufacturer to maintain and gain success. The Census Bureau of the U.S. Department of Commerce reported that online sales in 2005 grew 24.6 percent over 2004 to reach 86.3 billion dollars.

a. Channel conflict | b. Trade Symbols
c. Retail design | d. Store brand

9. The most important feature of a contract is that one party makes an _________ for an arrangement that another accepts. This can be called a 'concurrence of wills' or 'ad idem' (meeting of the minds) of two or more parties. The concept is somewhat contested.

a. ADTECH | b. ACNielsen
c. AMAX | d. Offer

10. _________ refers to when a retailer or wholesaler is 'tied' to purchase from a supplier on the understanding that no other distributor will be appointed or receive supplies in a given area. When the sales outlets are owned by the supplier, _________ is because of vertical integration, where the outlets are independent _________ is illegal due to the Restrictive Trade Practices Act, however, if it is registered and approved it is allowed.

_________ can be a barrier to entry, it can be defended on the grounds that it is beneficial to consumers as it can allow after sales service to be better.

a. ADTECH | b. ACNielsen
c. AMAX | d. Exclusive dealing

11. _________ is one of several anti-competitive practices forbidden in countries which have restricted market economies. For example, in Australia:

- Agreements involving competitors that involve restricting the supply of goods are prohibited if they have the purpose or effect of substantially lessening competition in a market in which the businesses operate.

'_________' Reference: The Competition Act, 2002 (India) S4-d.'_________' includes any agreement which restricts, or is likely to restrict, by any method the persons or classes of persons to whom goods are sold or from whom goods are bought

a. Jobbing house
b. Chief privacy officer
c. Mass market
d. Refusal to deal

1. _________ is an advertisement in which a particular product specifically mentions a competitor by name for the express purpose of showing why the competitor is inferior to the product naming it.

This should not be confused with parody advertisements, where a fictional product is being advertised for the purpose of poking fun at the particular advertisement, nor should it be confused with the use of a coined brand name for the purpose of comparing the product without actually naming an actual competitor. ('Wikipedia tastes better and is less filling than the Encyclopedia Galactica.')

In the 1980s, during what has been referred to as the cola wars, soft-drink manufacturer Pepsi ran a series of advertisements where people, caught on hidden camera, in a blind taste test, chose Pepsi over rival Coca-Cola.

a. Cost per conversion
b. Heavy-up
c. GL-70
d. Comparative advertising

2. _________ is one of the four elements of marketing mix. An organization or set of organizations (go-betweens) involved in the process of making a product or service available for use or consumption by a consumer or business user.

The other three parts of the marketing mix are product, pricing, and promotion.

a. Comparison-Shopping agent
b. Japan Advertising Photographers' Association
c. Distribution
d. Better Living Through Chemistry

3. In economics, an _________ is any good or commodity, transported from one country to another country in a legitimate fashion, typically for use in trade. _________ goods or services are provided to foreign consumers by domestic producers. _________ is an important part of international trade.

a. ADTECH
b. AMAX
c. ACNielsen
d. Export

4. _________s function as professionals who deal with trade, dealing in commodities that they do not produce themselves, in order to produce profit.

_________s can be of two types:

1. A wholesale _________ operates in the chain between producer and retail _________. Some wholesale _________s only organize the movement of goods rather than move the goods themselves.
2. A retail _________ or retailer, sells commodities to consumers (including businesses.) A shop owner is a retail _________.

A _________ class characterizes many pre-modern societies. Its status can range from high (even achieving titles like that of _________ prince or nabob) to low, such as in Chinese culture, due to the soiling capabilities of profiting from 'mere' trade, rather than from the labor of others reflected in agricultural produce, craftsmanship, and tribute.

In the United States, '_________' is defined (under the Uniform Commercial Code) as any person while engaged in a business or profession or a seller who deals regularly in the type of goods sold.

a. Retail loss prevention
b. RFM
c. Merchant
d. Trade credit

5. _________ wholesale represents a type of operation within the wholesale sector. Its main features are summarized best by the following definitions:

- _________ is a form of trade in which goods are sold from a wholesale warehouse operated either on a self-service basis, or on the basis of samples (with the customer selecting from specimen articles using a manual or computerized ordering system but not serving himself) or a combination of the two. Customers (retailers, professional users, caterers, institutional buyers, etc.) settle the invoice on the spot and in cash, and carry the goods away themselves.

- Though wholesalers buy primarily from manufacturers and sell mostly to retailers, industrial users and other wholesalers, they also perform many value added functions. The wholesaler, an intermediary, is used based on principles of specialisation and division of labour as well as contractual efficiency. (OECD -Organisation for Economic Cooperation and Development.)

a. Davie Brown Index
b. Containerization
c. Self branding
d. Cash and carry

6. A _________ is a party that mediates between a buyer and a seller. A _________ who also acts as a seller or as a buyer becomes a principal party to the deal. Distinguish agent: one who acts on behalf of a principal.

a. Broker
b. Power III
c. Spokesperson
d. 180SearchAssistant

7. _________ is subcontracting a process, such as product design or manufacturing, to a third-party company. The decision to outsource is often made in the interest of lowering cost or making better use of time and energy costs, redirecting or conserving energy directed at the competencies of a particular business, or to make more efficient use of land, labor, capital, (information) technology and resources. _________ became part of the business lexicon during the 1980s.

a. ACNielsen
b. Intangible assets
c. In-house
d. Outsourcing

8. _________ is the provision of service to customers before, during and after a purchase.

According to Turban et al., '_________ is a series of activities designed to enhance the level of customer satisfaction - that is, the feeling that a product or service has met the customer expectation.'

Its importance varies by product, industry and customer.

a. Facing
b. Customer experience
c. COPC Inc.
d. Customer service

9. The Oxford University Press defines _________ as 'marketing on a worldwide scale reconciling or taking commercial advantage of global operational differences, similarities and opportunities in order to meet global objectives.' Oxford University Press' Glossary of Marketing Terms.

Here are three reasons for the shift from domestic to _________ as given by the authors of the textbook, _________ Management--3rd Edition by Masaaki Kotabe and Kristiaan Helsen, 2004.

One of the product categories in which global competition has been easy to track is in U.S. automotive sales.

a. Diversity marketing
b. Guerrilla Marketing
c. Digital marketing
d. Global marketing

10. _________ is defined by the American _________ Association as the activity, set of institutions, and processes for creating, communicating, delivering, and exchanging offerings that have value for customers, clients, partners, and society at large. The term developed from the original meaning which referred literally to going to market, as in shopping, or going to a market to sell goods or services.

_________ practice tends to be seen as a creative industry, which includes advertising, distribution and selling.

a. Marketing
b. Product naming
c. Customer acquisition management
d. Marketing myopia

11. _________, also referred to as i-marketing, web marketing, online marketing is the marketing of products or services over the Internet.

The Internet has brought many unique benefits to marketing, one of which being lower costs for the distribution of information and media to a global audience. The interactive nature of _________, both in terms of providing instant response and eliciting responses, is a unique quality of the medium.

a. ADTECH
b. ACNielsen
c. AMAX
d. Internet marketing

12. In economics, business, retail, and accounting, a _________ is the value of money that has been used up to produce something, and hence is not available for use anymore. In economics, a _________ is an alternative that is given up as a result of a decision. In business, the _________ may be one of acquisition, in which case the amount of money expended to acquire it is counted as _________.

a. Variable cost
b. Fixed costs
c. Cost
d. Transaction cost

13. _________ refers to the structured transmission of data between organizations by electronic means. It is used to transfer electronic documents from one computer system to another (ie) from one trading partner to another trading partner. It is more than mere E-mail; for instance, organizations might replace bills of lading and even checks with appropriate _________ messages.

a. ADTECH
b. Electronic data interchange
c. ACNielsen
d. AMAX

14. _________ is a list for goods and materials held available in stock by a business. It is also used for a list of the contents of a household and for a list for testamentary purposes of the possessions of someone who has died. In accounting _________ is considered an asset.

a. Inventory
b. ACNielsen
c. Ending Inventory
d. ADTECH

15. _________ operations or facilities are commonly called 'distribution centers'. '_________' is the term generally used to describe the process or the work flow associated with the picking, packing and delivery of the packed item(s) to a shipping carrier.

a. AMAX
b. ACNielsen
c. ADTECH
d. Order processing

16. _________ refer to a collection of facts usually collected as the result of experience, observation or experiment or a set of premises. This may consist of numbers, words particularly as measurements or observations of a set of variables. _________ are often viewed as a lowest level of abstraction from which information and knowledge are derived.

a. Sample size
b. Mean
c. Pearson product-moment correlation coefficient
d. Data

17. _________ is an inventory strategy implemented to improve the return on investment of a business by reducing in-process inventory and its associated carrying costs. In order to achieve JIT the process must have signals of what is going on elsewhere within the process. This means that the process is often driven by a series of signals, which can be Kanban , that tell production processes when to make the next part.

a. Promotion
b. Clutter
c. Just-in-time
d. Personalization

18. The _________ is the level of inventory when a fresh order should be made with suppliers to bring the inventory up by the Economic order quantity (EOQ.)

The _________ for replenishment of stock occurs when the level of inventory drops down to zero. In view of instantaneous replenishment of stock the level of inventory jumps to the original level from zero level.

a. Net realisable value
b. Stock forecast
c. Stock obsolescence
d. Reorder point

19. _________ is a term used by inventory specialists to describe a level of stock that is maintained below the cycle stock to buffer against stockouts. _________ exists to counter uncertainties in supply and demand. _________ is defined as extra units of inventory carried as protection against possible stockouts.

a. Price-weighted
b. Cross-docking
c. Product support
d. Safety stock

20. _________ is a system of intermodal freight transport using standard intermodal containers that are standardised by the International Organization for Standardization (ISO.) These can be loaded and sealed intact onto container ships, railroad cars, planes, and trucks.

a. Scientific controls
b. BeyondROI
c. Rebate
d. Containerization

21. A _________ for a set of products is a warehouse or other specialized building, often with refrigeration or air conditioning, which is stocked with products (goods) to be re-distributed to retailers, wholesalers or directly to consumers. A _________ is a principle part, the 'order processing' element, of the entire 'order fulfillment' process. _________s are usually thought of as being 'demand driven'.

a. Power III
b. Distribution center
c. 6-3-5 Brainwriting
d. 180SearchAssistant

22. A _________ is a commercial building for storage of goods. _________s are used by manufacturers, importers, exporters, wholesalers, transport businesses, customs, etc. They are usually large plain buildings in industrial areas of cities and towns.

a. 180SearchAssistant
b. 6-3-5 Brainwriting
c. Power III
d. Warehouse

23. _________ in economics and business is the result of an exchange and from that trade we assign a numerical monetary value to a good, service or asset. If I trade 4 apples for an orange, the _________ of an orange is 4 - apples. Inversely, the _________ of an apple is 1/4 oranges.

a. Discounts and allowances
b. Contribution margin-based pricing
c. Pricing
d. Price

24. A _________ is a process that can allow an organization to concentrate its limited resources on the greatest opportunities to increase sales and achieve a sustainable competitive advantage. A _________ should be centered around the key concept that customer satisfaction is the main goal.

A _________ is most effective when it is an integral component of corporate strategy, defining how the organization will successfully engage customers, prospects, and competitors in the market arena.

a. Societal marketing
b. Psychographic
c. Cyberdoc
d. Marketing strategy

1. _________ consists of the sale of goods or merchandise from a fixed location, such as a department store or kiosk in small or individual lots for direct consumption by the purchaser. _________ may include subordinated services, such as delivery. Purchasers may be individuals or businesses.

a. Charity shop
b. Retailing
c. Warehouse store
d. Thrifting

2. _________ is defined by the American _________ Association as the activity, set of institutions, and processes for creating, communicating, delivering, and exchanging offerings that have value for customers, clients, partners, and society at large. The term developed from the original meaning which referred literally to going to market, as in shopping, or going to a market to sell goods or services.

_________ practice tends to be seen as a creative industry, which includes advertising, distribution and selling.

a. Marketing myopia
b. Customer acquisition management
c. Marketing
d. Product naming

3. A _________ is a retail establishment which specializes in selling a wide range of products without a single predominant merchandise line. _________s usually sell products including apparel, furniture, appliances, electronics, and additionally select other lines of products such as paint, hardware, toiletries, cosmetics, photographic equipment, jewelery, toys, and sporting goods. Certain _________s are further classified as discount _________s.

a. 180SearchAssistant
b. 6-3-5 Brainwriting
c. Department store
d. Power III

4. A _________ is a type of department store, which sell products at prices lower than those asked by traditional retail outlets. Most discount department stores offer wide assortments of goods; others specialize in such merchandise as jewelry, electronic equipment, or electrical appliances. _________s are not dollar stores, which sell goods at a dollar or less.

a. Strip mall
b. Sales per unit area
c. Gruen transfer
d. Discount store

5. In commerce, a _________ is a superstore which combines a supermarket and a department store. The result is a very large retail facility which carries an enormous range of products under one roof, including full lines of groceries and general merchandise. In theory, _________s allow customers to satisfy all their routine weekly shopping needs in one trip.

a. 180SearchAssistant
b. 6-3-5 Brainwriting
c. Power III
d. Hypermarket

6. A _________ is a commercial building for storage of goods. _________s are used by manufacturers, importers, exporters, wholesalers, transport businesses, customs, etc. They are usually large plain buildings in industrial areas of cities and towns.

a. Power III
b. 6-3-5 Brainwriting
c. Warehouse
d. 180SearchAssistant

7. A _________ is a retail store, usually selling a wide variety of merchandise, in which customers pay annual membership fees in order to shop. The clubs are able to keep prices low due to the no-frills format of the stores. In addition, customers are required to buy large, wholesale quantities of the store's products, which makes these clubs attractive to both bargain hunters and small business owners.

a. Warehouse club
b. Consignment
c. Power centre
d. Self service

8. _________ is a term used in marketing and strategic management to describe a product, service, brand, or company that has such a distinct sustainable competitive advantage that competing firms find it almost impossible to operate profitably in that industry. The existence of a _________ will eliminate almost all market entities, whether real or virtual. Many existing firms will leave the industry, thereby increasing the industry's concentration ratio.

a. Power III
b. 180SearchAssistant
c. 6-3-5 Brainwriting
d. Category killer

9. _________ is a sub-discipline and type of marketing. There are two main definitional characteristics which distinguish it from other types of marketing. The first is that it attempts to send its messages directly to consumers, without the use of intervening media.

a. Database marketing
b. Direct Marketing Associations
c. Power III
d. Direct marketing

10. _________ is a retail channel for the distribution of goods and services. At a basic level it may be defined as marketing and selling products, direct to consumers away from a fixed retail location. Sales are typically made through party plan, one to one demonstrations, and other personal contact arrangements.

a. 180SearchAssistant
b. 6-3-5 Brainwriting
c. Power III
d. Direct selling

11. _________ is a sales technique in which a salesperson walks from one door of a house to another trying to sell a product or service to the general public. A variant of this involves cold calling first, when another sales representative attempts to gain agreement that a salesperson should visit. _________ selling is usually conducted in the afternoon hours, when the majority of people are at home.

a. Marketing management
b. Performance-based advertising
c. Fast moving consumer goods
d. Door-to-door

12. _________ commonly refers to the electronic retailing / _________ channels industry, which includes such billion dollar companies as Home shoppingN, QVC, eBay, ShopNBC, Buy.com, and Amazon.com. _________ allows consumers to shop for goods while in the privacy of their own home, as opposed to traditional shopping, which requires you to visit brick and mortar stores and shopping malls.

The _________ / electronic retailing industry was created in 1977 when small market radio talk show host Bob Circosta was asked to sell avocado-green-colored can openers live on the air by station owner Bud Paxson when an advertiser traded 112 units of product instead of paying his advertising bill.

a. 180SearchAssistant
b. Home shopping
c. Power III
d. 6-3-5 Brainwriting

13. _________ is a method of direct marketing in which a salesperson solicits to prospective customers to buy products or services, either over the phone or through a subsequent face to face or Web conferencing appointment scheduled during the call.

_________ can also include recorded sales pitches programmed to be played over the phone via automatic dialing. _________ has come under fire in recent years, being viewed as an annoyance by many.

a. Phishing
b. Directory Harvest Attack
c. Joe job
d. Telemarketing

14. _________ is the state or fact of exclusive rights and control over property, which may be an object, land/real estate, or some other kind of property (like government-granted monopolies collectively referred to as intellectual property.) It is embodied in an _________ right also referred to as title.

_________ is the key building block in the development of the capitalist socio-economic system.

a. ACNielsen
b. ADTECH
c. Ownership
d. AMAX

15. _________ is the examining of goods or services from retailers with the intent to purchase at that time. _________ is an activity of selection and/or purchase. In some contexts it is considered a leisure activity as well as an economic one.

a. Hawkers
b. Discount store
c. Khodebshchik
d. Shopping

16. The Oxford University Press defines _________ as 'marketing on a worldwide scale reconciling or taking commercial advantage of global operational differences, similarities and opportunities in order to meet global objectives.' Oxford University Press' Glossary of Marketing Terms.

Here are three reasons for the shift from domestic to _________ as given by the authors of the textbook, _________ Management--3rd Edition by Masaaki Kotabe and Kristiaan Helsen, 2004.

One of the product categories in which global competition has been easy to track is in U.S. automotive sales.

a. Diversity marketing
b. Digital marketing
c. Guerrilla Marketing
d. Global marketing

17. _________, also referred to as i-marketing, web marketing, online marketing is the marketing of products or services over the Internet.

The Internet has brought many unique benefits to marketing, one of which being lower costs for the distribution of information and media to a global audience. The interactive nature of _________, both in terms of providing instant response and eliciting responses, is a unique quality of the medium.

a. ADTECH
b. Internet marketing
c. AMAX
d. ACNielsen

18. _________ refers to the methods of practicing and using another person's philosophy of business. The franchisor grants the independent operator the right to distribute its products, techniques, and trademarks for a percentage of gross monthly sales and a royalty fee. Various tangibles and intangibles such as national or international advertising, training, and other support services are commonly made available by the franchisor.

a. Franchise fee
b. 180SearchAssistant
c. Power III
d. Franchising

19. In marketing, _________ has come to mean the process by which marketers try to create an image or identity in the minds of their target market for its product, brand, or organization. It is the 'relative competitive comparison' their product occupies in a given market as perceived by the target market.

Re-_________ involves changing the identity of a product, relative to the identity of competing products, in the collective minds of the target market.

a. Moratorium
b. GE matrix
c. Positioning
d. Containerization

20. _________ refers to the methods, practices and operations conducted to promote and sustain certain categories of commercial activity. The term is understood to have different specific meanings depending on the context. Merchandise is a sale goods at a store

In marketing, one of the definitions of _________ is the practice in which the brand or image from one product or service is used to sell another.

a. Marketing communication
b. New Media Strategies
c. Word of mouth
d. Merchandising

1. _________ , according to The American Marketing Association, is 'a planning process designed to assure that all brand contacts received by a customer or prospect for a product, service, or organization are relevant to that person and consistent over time.' (Marketing Power Dictionary)

_________ is a term used to describe a holistic approach to marketing. It aims to ensure consistency of message and the complementary use of media. The concept includes online and offline marketing channels.

a. Integrated marketing communications
b. AMAX
c. ACNielsen
d. ADTECH

2. _________ is defined by the American _________ Association as the activity, set of institutions, and processes for creating, communicating, delivering, and exchanging offerings that have value for customers, clients, partners, and society at large. The term developed from the original meaning which referred literally to going to market, as in shopping, or going to a market to sell goods or services.

_________ practice tends to be seen as a creative industry, which includes advertising, distribution and selling.

a. Product naming
b. Marketing myopia
c. Customer acquisition management
d. Marketing

3. _________ refers to messages and related media used to communicate with a market. Those who practice advertising, branding, direct marketing, graphic design, marketing, packaging, promotion, publicity, sponsorship, public relations, sales, sales promotion and online marketing are termed marketing communicators, _________ managers, or more briefly as marcom managers.

a. Merchandise
b. Marketing communication
c. Merchandising
d. Sales promotion

4. _________ involves disseminating information about a product, product line, brand, or company. It is one of the four key aspects of the marketing mix. (The other three elements are product marketing, pricing, and distribution). P>_________ is generally sub-divided into two parts:

- Above the line _________: Promotion in the media (e.g. TV, radio, newspapers, Internet and Mobile Phones) in which the advertiser pays an advertising agency to place the ad
- Below the line _________: All other _________. Much of this is intended to be subtle enough for the consumer to be unaware that _________ is taking place. E.g. sponsorship, product placement, endorsements, sales _________, merchandising, direct mail, personal selling, public relations, trade shows

a. Promotion
b. Cashmere Agency
c. Davie Brown Index
d. Bottling lines

5. _________ is the reverse of encoding, which is the process of transforming information from one format into another. Information about _________ can be found in the following:

- Digital-to-analog converter, the use of analog circuit for _________ operations
- Code, a rule for converting a piece of information into another form or representation
- Code (cryptography), a method used to transform a message into an obscured form
- _________
- _________ methods, methods in communication theory for _________ codewords sent over a noisy channel
- Digital signal processing, the study of signals in a digital representation and the processing methods of these signals
- Word _________, the use of phonics to decipher print patterns and translate them into the sounds of language
- deCODE genetics

.

a. 180SearchAssistant
b. Decoding
c. Power III
d. 6-3-5 Brainwriting

6. _________ describes the situation when output from (or information about the result of) an event or phenomenon in the past will influence the same event/phenomenon in the present or future. When an event is part of a chain of cause-and-effect that forms a circuit or loop, then the event is said to 'feed back' into itself.

_________ is also a synonym for:

- _________ Signal; the information about the initial event that is the basis for subsequent modification of the event.
- _________ Loop; the causal path that leads from the initial generation of the _________ signal to the subsequent modification of the event.

_________ is a mechanism, process or signal that is looped back to control a system within itself. Such a loop is called a _________ loop.

a. 180SearchAssistant
b. 6-3-5 Brainwriting
c. Power III
d. Feedback

7. In economics, _________ is the desire to own something and the ability to pay for it. The term _________ signifies the ability or the willingness to buy a particular commodity at a given point of time .

.

a. Discretionary spending
b. Market dominance
c. Market system
d. Demand

8. _________ is a rivalry between individuals, groups, nations for territory, a niche, or allocation of resources. It arises whenever two or more parties strive for a goal which cannot be shared. _________ occurs naturally between living organisms which co-exist in the same environment.

a. Price fixing
b. Price competition
c. Competition
d. Non-price competition

9. A _________ is a company or individual that purchases goods or services with the intention of reselling them rather than consuming or using them. This is usually done for profit (but could be resold at a loss.) One example can be found in the industry of telecommunications, where companies buy excess amounts of transmission capacity or call time from other carriers and resell it to smaller carriers.

a. Discontinuation
b. Value-based pricing
c. Jobbing house
d. Reseller

10. _________ is a form of communication that typically attempts to persuade potential customers to purchase or to consume more of a particular brand of product or service. 'While now central to the contemporary global economy and the reproduction of global production networks, it is only quite recently that _________ has been more than a marginal influence on patterns of sales and production. The formation of modern _________ was intimately bound up with the emergence of new forms of monopoly capitalism around the end of the 19th and beginning of the 20th century as one element in corporate strategies to create, organize and where possible control markets, especially for mass produced consumer goods.

a. ADTECH
b. AMAX
c. Advertising
d. ACNielsen

11. _________ is the practice of managing the flow of information between an organization and its publics. _________ - often referred to as _________ - gains an organization or individual exposure to their audiences using topics of public interest and news items that do not require direct payment. Because _________ places exposure in credible third-party outlets, it offers a third-party legitimacy that advertising does not have.

a. Power III
b. Symbolic analysis
c. Graphic communication
d. Public relations

12. _________ is an unconventional system of promotions that relies on time, energy and imagination rather than a big marketing budget. Typically, _________ tactics are unexpected and unconventional; consumers are targeted in unexpected places, which can make the idea that's being marketed memorable, generate buzz, and even spread virally. The term was coined and defined by Jay Conrad Levinson in his 1984 book _________.

a. Cause-related Marketing
b. Diversity marketing
c. Digital marketing
d. Guerrilla marketing

13. _________ is one of the four aspects of promotional mix. (The other three parts of the promotional mix are advertising, personal selling, and publicity/public relations.) Media and non-media marketing communication are employed for a pre-determined, limited time to increase consumer demand, stimulate market demand or improve product availability.

a. New Media Strategies
b. Merchandise
c. Marketing communication
d. Sales promotion

14. _________ or simply buzz is a term used in word-of-mouth marketing. The interaction of consumers and users of a product or service serve to amplify the original marketing message.

Some describe buzz as a form of hype among consumers, a vague but positive association, excitement, or anticipation about a product or service.

a. Consumer confidence
b. Consumption smoothing
c. Multidimensional scaling
d. Marketing buzz

15. _________ is a business term meaning the market segment to which a particular good or service is marketed. It is mainly defined by age, gender, geography, socio-economic grouping, technographic, or any other combination of demographics. It is generally studied and mapped by an organization through lists and reports containing demographic information that may have an effect on the marketing of key products or services.

a. Brando
b. Market specialization
c. Category Development Index
d. Distribution

16. _________ and viral advertising refer to marketing techniques that use pre-existing social networks to produce increases in brand awareness or to achieve other marketing objectives (such as product sales) through self-replicating viral processes, analogous to the spread of pathological and computer viruses. It can be word-of-mouth delivered or enhanced by the network effects of the Internet. Viral promotions may take the form of video clips, interactive Flash games, advergames, ebooks, brandable software, images, or even text messages.

a. Power III
b. 180SearchAssistant
c. New Media Marketing
d. Viral marketing

17. Human beings are also considered to be _________ because they have the ability to change raw materials into valuable _________. The term Human _________ can also be defined as the skills, energies, talents, abilities and knowledge that are used for the production of goods or the rendering of services. While taking into account human beings as _________, the following things have to be kept in mind:

- The size of the population
- The capabilities of the individuals in that population

Many _________ cannot be consumed in their original form. They have to be processed in order to change them into more usable commodities.

a. 180SearchAssistant
b. 6-3-5 Brainwriting
c. Power III
d. Resources

18. In economics, business, retail, and accounting, a _________ is the value of money that has been used up to produce something, and hence is not available for use anymore. In economics, a _________ is an alternative that is given up as a result of a decision. In business, the _________ may be one of acquisition, in which case the amount of money expended to acquire it is counted as _________.

a. Fixed costs
b. Transaction cost
c. Variable cost
d. Cost

19. The break-even point for a product is the point where total revenue received equals the total costs associated with the sale of the product (TR=TC.) A break-even point is typically calculated in order for businesses to determine if it would be profitable to sell a proposed product, as opposed to attempting to modify an existing product instead so it can be made lucrative. _________ can also be used to analyse the potential profitability of an expenditure in a sales-based business.

In _________, margin of safety is how much output or sales level can fall before a business reaches its break-even point (BEP).

a. Pay Per Sale
b. Price skimming
c. Break even analysis
d. Contribution margin-based pricing

20. The business terms _________ and pull originated in the logistic and supply chain management, but are also widely used in marketing.

A _________-pull-system in business describes the move of a product or information between two subjects. On markets the consumers usually 'pulls' the goods or information they demand for their needs, while the offerers or suppliers '_________es' them toward the consumers.

a. Push
b. Manufacturers' representatives
c. Gold Key Matching Service
d. Completely randomized designs

21. _________ in economics and business is the result of an exchange and from that trade we assign a numerical monetary value to a good, service or asset. If I trade 4 apples for an orange, the _________ of an orange is 4 - apples. Inversely, the _________ of an apple is 1/4 oranges.

a. Contribution margin-based pricing
b. Discounts and allowances
c. Pricing
d. Price

22. The philosophy of _________ holds that the only thing that exists is matter, and is considered a form of physicalism. Fundamentally, all things are composed of material and all phenomena (including consciousness) are the result of material interactions; therefore, matter is the only substance. As a theory, _________ belongs to the class of monist ontology.

a. 180SearchAssistant
b. Power III
c. 6-3-5 Brainwriting
d. Materialism

1. _________ is a form of communication that typically attempts to persuade potential customers to purchase or to consume more of a particular brand of product or service. 'While now central to the contemporary global economy and the reproduction of global production networks, it is only quite recently that _________ has been more than a marginal influence on patterns of sales and production. The formation of modern _________ was intimately bound up with the emergence of new forms of monopoly capitalism around the end of the 19th and beginning of the 20th century as one element in corporate strategies to create, organize and where possible control markets, especially for mass produced consumer goods.

a. ACNielsen
b. ADTECH
c. AMAX
d. Advertising

2. _________ is the pursuit of influencing outcomes -- including public-policy and resource allocation decisions within political, economic, and social systems and institutions -- that directly affect people's current lives. (Cohen, 2001)

Therefore, _________ can be seen as a deliberate process of speaking out on issues of concern in order to exert some influence on behalf of ideas or persons. Based on this definition, Cohen (2001) states that 'ideologues of all persuasions advocate' to bring a change in people's lives.

a. ADTECH
b. AMAX
c. ACNielsen
d. Advocacy

3. In grammar, the _________ is the form of an adjective or adverb which denotes the degree or grade by which a person, thing and is used in this context with a subordinating conjunction, such as than, as...as, etc.

The structure of a _________ in English consists normally of the positive form of the adjective or adverb, plus the suffix -er e.g. 'he is taller than his father is', or 'the village is less picturesque than the town nearby'.

a. Power III
b. 180SearchAssistant
c. 6-3-5 Brainwriting
d. Comparative

4. _________ is an advertisement in which a particular product specifically mentions a competitor by name for the express purpose of showing why the competitor is inferior to the product naming it.

This should not be confused with parody advertisements, where a fictional product is being advertised for the purpose of poking fun at the particular advertisement, nor should it be confused with the use of a coined brand name for the purpose of comparing the product without actually naming an actual competitor. ('Wikipedia tastes better and is less filling than the Encyclopedia Galactica.')

In the 1980s, during what has been referred to as the cola wars, soft-drink manufacturer Pepsi ran a series of advertisements where people, caught on hidden camera, in a blind taste test, chose Pepsi over rival Coca-Cola.

a. Cost per conversion
b. Heavy-up
c. GL-70
d. Comparative advertising

5. Competitiveness is a comparative concept of the ability and performance of a firm, sub-sector or country to sell and supply goods and/or services in a given market. Although widely used in economics and business management, the usefulness of the concept, particularly in the context of national competitiveness, is vigorously disputed by economists, such as Paul Krugman .

The term may also be applied to markets, where it is used to refer to the extent to which the market structure may be regarded as perfectly _________.

a. Customs union
b. Competitive
c. Geographical pricing
d. Free trade zone

6. An _________ is a series of advertisement messages that share a single idea and theme which make up an integrated marketing communication (IMC.) _________s appear in different media across a specific time frame.

The critical part of making an _________ is determining a campaign theme, as it sets the tone for the individual advertisements and other forms of marketing communications that will be used.

a. Advertising campaign
b. ADTECH
c. AMAX
d. ACNielsen

7. In operant conditioning, _________ occurs when an event following a response causes an increase in the probability of that response occurring in the future. Response strength can be assessed by measures such as the frequency with which the response is made (for example, a pigeon may peck a key more times in the session), or the speed with which it is made (for example, a rat may run a maze faster.) The environment change contingent upon the response is called a reinforcer.

a. Generic brands
b. Reinforcement
c. Completely randomized designs
d. Relationship Management Application

8. In marketing and advertising, a _________ usually an advertising campaign, is aimed at appealing to. A _________ can be people of a certain age group, gender, marital status, etc. (ex: teenagers, females, single people, etc.)

a. Targeted advertising
b. National brand
c. Target audience
d. Brand Development Index

9. In economics, business, retail, and accounting, a _________ is the value of money that has been used up to produce something, and hence is not available for use anymore. In economics, a _________ is an alternative that is given up as a result of a decision. In business, the _________ may be one of acquisition, in which case the amount of money expended to acquire it is counted as _________.

a. Transaction cost
b. Cost
c. Variable cost
d. Fixed costs

10. Advertising mail junk mail is the delivery of advertising material to recipients of postal mail. The delivery of advertising mail forms a large and growing service for many postal services, and _________ marketing forms a significant portion of the direct marketing industry. Some organizations attempt to help people opt-out of receiving advertising mail, in many cases motivated by a concern over its negative environmental impact.

a. Phishing
b. Direct mail
c. Telemarketing
d. Directory Harvest Attack

11. _________ is the management of the flow of goods, information and other resources, including energy and people, between the point of origin and the point of consumption in order to meet the requirements of consumers (frequently, and originally, military organizations.) _________ involves the integration of information, transportation, inventory, warehousing, material-handling, and packaging. _________ is a channel of the supply chain which adds the value of time and place utility.

a. 6-3-5 Brainwriting
b. Power III
c. 180SearchAssistant
d. Logistics

12. _________ is defined by the American _________ Association as the activity, set of institutions, and processes for creating, communicating, delivering, and exchanging offerings that have value for customers, clients, partners, and society at large. The term developed from the original meaning which referred literally to going to market, as in shopping, or going to a market to sell goods or services.

_________ practice tends to be seen as a creative industry, which includes advertising, distribution and selling.

a. Product naming
b. Marketing myopia
c. Customer acquisition management
d. Marketing

13. _________ in economics and business is the result of an exchange and from that trade we assign a numerical monetary value to a good, service or asset. If I trade 4 apples for an orange, the _________ of an orange is 4 - apples. Inversely, the _________ of an apple is 1/4 oranges.

a. Contribution margin-based pricing
b. Discounts and allowances
c. Pricing
d. Price

14. _________ is the use of sexual or erotic imagery in advertising to draw interest to a particular product, for purpose of sale. A feature of _________ is that the imagery used, such as that of a pretty woman, typically has no connection to the product being advertised. The purpose of the imagery is to attract attention of the potential customer or user.

a. Power III
b. 6-3-5 Brainwriting
c. 180SearchAssistant
d. Sex in advertising

15. _________ is a broad label that refers to any individuals or households that use goods and services generated within the economy. The concept of a _________ is used in different contexts, so that the usage and significance of the term may vary.

A _________ is a person who uses any product or service.

a. 6-3-5 Brainwriting
b. Consumer
c. 180SearchAssistant
d. Power III

16. _________ is systematic determination of merit, worth, and significance of something or someone using criteria against a set of standards. _________ often is used to characterize and appraise subjects of interest in a wide range of human enterprises, including the arts, criminal justice, foundations and non-profit organizations, government, health care, and other human services.

Depending on the topic of interest, there are professional groups which look to the quality and rigor of the _________ process.

a. ACNielsen
b. ADTECH
c. AMAX
d. Evaluation

17. _________ is the practice of managing the flow of information between an organization and its publics. _________ - often referred to as _________ - gains an organization or individual exposure to their audiences using topics of public interest and news items that do not require direct payment. Because _________ places exposure in credible third-party outlets, it offers a third-party legitimacy that advertising does not have.

a. Public relations
b. Graphic communication
c. Power III
d. Symbolic analysis

18. _________ is the deliberate attempt to manage the public's perception of a subject. The subjects of _________ include people (for example, politicians and performing artists), goods and services, organizations of all kinds, and works of art or entertainment.

From a marketing perspective, _________ is one component of promotion.

a. Pearson's chi-square
b. Little value placed on potential benefits
c. Brando
d. Publicity

19. The general definition of an _________ is an evaluation of a person, organization, system, process, project or product. _________s are performed to ascertain the validity and reliability of information; also to provide an assessment of a system's internal control. The goal of an _________ is to express an opinion on the person/organization/system (etc) in question, under evaluation based on work done on a test basis.

a. ADTECH
b. AMAX
c. Audit
d. ACNielsen

20. _________ describes the processes and activities that need to take place to characterise and monitor the quality of the environment. _________ is used in the preparation of environmental impact assessments, as well as in many circumstances in which human activities carry a risk of harmful effects on the natural environment. All monitoring strategies and programmes have reasons and justifications which are often designed to establish the current status of an environment or to establish trends in environmental parameters.

a. ADTECH
b. Environmental monitoring
c. AMAX
d. ACNielsen

21. An alternative phenomenon is the creation of external _________ by groups or individuals independent of the accountable organisation and typically without its encouragement. External _________ thus also attempt to blur the boundaries between organisations and society and to establish social accounting as a fluid two-way communication process. Companies are sought to be held accountable regardless of their approval.

a. 180SearchAssistant
b. 6-3-5 Brainwriting
c. Power III
d. Social audits

1. _________ is the physical search for minerals, fossils, precious metals or mineral specimens, and is also known as fossicking.

_________ is synonymous in some ways with mineral exploration which is an organised, large scale and at least semi-scientific effort undertaken by mineral resource companies to find commercially viable ore deposits. To actually be considered a prospector you must become registered as a professional prospector.

a. 6-3-5 Brainwriting
b. Power III
c. 180SearchAssistant
d. Prospecting

2. _________ is a term used by inventory specialists to describe a level of stock that is maintained below the cycle stock to buffer against stockouts. _________ exists to counter uncertainties in supply and demand. _________ is defined as extra units of inventory carried as protection against possible stockouts.

a. Cross-docking
b. Product support
c. Price-weighted
d. Safety stock

3. _________ involves disseminating information about a product, product line, brand, or company. It is one of the four key aspects of the marketing mix. (The other three elements are product marketing, pricing, and distribution). P>_________ is generally sub-divided into two parts:

- Above the line _________: Promotion in the media (e.g. TV, radio, newspapers, Internet and Mobile Phones) in which the advertiser pays an advertising agency to place the ad
- Below the line _________: All other _________. Much of this is intended to be subtle enough for the consumer to be unaware that _________ is taking place. E.g. sponsorship, product placement, endorsements, sales _________, merchandising, direct mail, personal selling, public relations, trade shows

a. Bottling lines
b. Davie Brown Index
c. Cashmere Agency
d. Promotion

4. _________ is systematic determination of merit, worth, and significance of something or someone using criteria against a set of standards. _________ often is used to characterize and appraise subjects of interest in a wide range of human enterprises, including the arts, criminal justice, foundations and non-profit organizations, government, health care, and other human services.

Depending on the topic of interest, there are professional groups which look to the quality and rigor of the _________ process.

a. AMAX
b. ACNielsen
c. ADTECH
d. Evaluation

5. _________ is a form of communication that typically attempts to persuade potential customers to purchase or to consume more of a particular brand of product or service. 'While now central to the contemporary global economy and the reproduction of global production networks, it is only quite recently that _________ has been more than a marginal influence on patterns of sales and production. The formation of modern _________ was intimately bound up with the emergence of new forms of monopoly capitalism around the end of the 19th and beginning of the 20th century as one element in corporate strategies to create, organize and where possible control markets, especially for mass produced consumer goods.

a. ADTECH
b. AMAX
c. ACNielsen
d. Advertising

6. _________ is defined by the American _________ Association as the activity, set of institutions, and processes for creating, communicating, delivering, and exchanging offerings that have value for customers, clients, partners, and society at large. The term developed from the original meaning which referred literally to going to market, as in shopping, or going to a market to sell goods or services.

_________ practice tends to be seen as a creative industry, which includes advertising, distribution and selling.

a. Product naming
b. Marketing
c. Customer acquisition management
d. Marketing myopia

7. _________ is one of the four aspects of promotional mix. (The other three parts of the promotional mix are advertising, personal selling, and publicity/public relations.) Media and non-media marketing communication are employed for a pre-determined, limited time to increase consumer demand, stimulate market demand or improve product availability.

a. Marketing communication
b. Merchandise
c. New Media Strategies
d. Sales promotion

8. _________ in economics and business is the result of an exchange and from that trade we assign a numerical monetary value to a good, service or asset. If I trade 4 apples for an orange, the _________ of an orange is 4 - apples. Inversely, the _________ of an apple is 1/4 oranges.

a. Discounts and allowances
b. Price
c. Contribution margin-based pricing
d. Pricing

9. _________ is a broad label that refers to any individuals or households that use goods and services generated within the economy. The concept of a _________ is used in different contexts, so that the usage and significance of the term may vary.

A _________ is a person who uses any product or service.

a. 6-3-5 Brainwriting
b. Consumer
c. Power III
d. 180SearchAssistant

10. _________ can be regarded as an outcome of mental processes (cognitive process) leading to the selection of a course of action among several alternatives. Every _________ process produces a final choice. The output can be an action or an opinion of choice.

a. 180SearchAssistant
b. Decision making
c. Power III
d. 6-3-5 Brainwriting

11. In marketing a _________ is a ticket or document that can be exchanged for a financial discount or rebate when purchasing a product. Customarily, _________s are issued by manufacturers of consumer packaged goods or by retailers, to be used in retail stores as a part of sales promotions. They are often widely distributed through mail, magazines, newspapers, the Internet, and mobile devices such as cell phones.

a. Marketing communication
b. Coupon
c. Merchandising
d. Merchandise

12. In economics and sociology, an _________ is any factor (financial or non-financial) that enables or motivates a particular course of action, or counts as a reason for preferring one choice to the alternatives. It is an expectation that encourages people to behave in a certain way. Since human beings are purposeful creatures, the study of _________ structures is central to the study of all economic activity (both in terms of individual decision-making and in terms of co-operation and competition within a larger institutional structure.)

a. ADTECH
b. ACNielsen
c. AMAX
d. Incentive

13. The Oxford University Press defines _________ as 'marketing on a worldwide scale reconciling or taking commercial advantage of global operational differences, similarities and opportunities in order to meet global objectives.' Oxford University Press' Glossary of Marketing Terms.

Here are three reasons for the shift from domestic to _________ as given by the authors of the textbook, _________ Management--3rd Edition by Masaaki Kotabe and Kristiaan Helsen, 2004.

One of the product categories in which global competition has been easy to track is in U.S. automotive sales.

a. Diversity marketing
b. Digital marketing
c. Guerrilla Marketing
d. Global marketing

14. _________ is anything that is generally accepted as payment for goods and services and repayment of debts. The main uses of _________ are as a medium of exchange, a unit of account, and a store of value. Some authors explicitly require _________ to be a standard of deferred payment.

a. Law of supply
b. Money
c. Microeconomics
d. Leading indicator

15. A _________ is an amount paid by way of reduction, return, or refund on what has already been paid or contributed. It is a type of sales promotion marketers use primarily as incentives or supplements to product sales. The mail-in _________ is the most common.

a. Personalization
b. Strand
c. Lifestyle city
d. Rebate

16. _________, also referred to as i-marketing, web marketing, online marketing is the marketing of products or services over the Internet.

The Internet has brought many unique benefits to marketing, one of which being lower costs for the distribution of information and media to a global audience. The interactive nature of _________, both in terms of providing instant response and eliciting responses, is a unique quality of the medium.

a. AMAX
b. ACNielsen
c. ADTECH
d. Internet marketing

17. _________ is that part of statistical practice concerned with the selection of individual observations intended to yield some knowledge about a population of concern, especially for the purposes of statistical inference. Each observation measures one or more properties (weight, location, etc.) of an observable entity enumerated to distinguish objects or individuals.

a. Sports Marketing Group
b. AStore
c. Richard Buckminster 'Bucky' Fuller
d. Sampling

18. The most important feature of a contract is that one party makes an _________ for an arrangement that another accepts. This can be called a 'concurrence of wills' or 'ad idem' (meeting of the minds) of two or more parties. The concept is somewhat contested.

a. ADTECH
b. Offer
c. ACNielsen
d. AMAX

19. Merchandising refers to the methods, practices and operations conducted to promote and sustain certain categories of commercial activity. The term is understood to have different specific meanings depending on the context. _________ is a sale goods at a store

In marketing, one of the definitions of merchandising is the practice in which the brand or image from one product or service is used to sell another.

a. Merchandising
b. New Media Strategies
c. Sales promotion
d. Merchandise

20. In the United States consumer sales promotions known as _________ or simply sweeps (both single and plural) have become associated with marketing promotions targeted toward both generating enthusiasm and providing incentive reactions among customers by enticing consumers to submit free entries into drawings of chance (and not skill) that are tied to product or service awareness wherein the featured prizes are given away by sponsoring companies. Prizes can vary in value from less than one dollar to more than one million U.S. dollars and can be in the form of cash, cars, homes, electronics, etc.

_________ frequently have eligibility limited by international, national, state, local, or other geographical factors.

a. Commercial planning
b. Market segment
c. Claritas Prizm
d. Sweepstakes

21. A _________ is defined by the International Co-operative Alliance's Statement on the Co-operative Identity as an autonomous association of persons united voluntarily to meet their common economic, social, and cultural needs and aspirations through a jointly-owned and democratically-controlled enterprise. It is a business organization owned and operated by a group of individuals for their mutual benefit. A _________ may also be defined as a business owned and controlled equally by the people who use its services or who work at it.

a. Power III
b. 180SearchAssistant
c. 6-3-5 Brainwriting
d. Cooperative

22. The business terms _________ and pull originated in the logistic and supply chain management, but are also widely used in marketing.

A _________-pull-system in business describes the move of a product or information between two subjects. On markets the consumers usually 'pulls' the goods or information they demand for their needs, while the offerers or suppliers '_________es' them toward the consumers.

a. Manufacturers' representatives
b. Gold Key Matching Service
c. Completely randomized designs
d. Push

23. _________ is a rivalry between individuals, groups, nations for territory, a niche, or allocation of resources. It arises whenever two or more parties strive for a goal which cannot be shared. _________ occurs naturally between living organisms which co-exist in the same environment.

a. Price fixing
b. Non-price competition
c. Competition
d. Price competition

1. _________ is one of the four Ps of the marketing mix. The other three aspects are product, promotion, and place. It is also a key variable in microeconomic price allocation theory.

a. Competitor indexing
b. Price
c. Relationship based pricing
d. Pricing

2. _________ is a type of trade in which goods or services are directly exchanged for other goods and/or services, without the use of money. It can be bilateral or multilateral, and usually exists parallel to monetary systems in most developed countries, though to a very limited extent. _________ usually replaces money as the method of exchange in times of monetary crisis, when the currency is unstable and devalued by hyperinflation.

a. Barter
b. Mixed economy
c. Black market
d. Market economy

3. A _________ is the fee paid by a traveler allowing him or her to make use of a public transport system: rail, bus, taxi, etc. In the case of air transport, the term airfare is often used.

The _________ paid is a contribution to the operational costs of the transport system involved, either partial (as is frequently the case with publicly supported systems) or total.

a. Power III
b. 6-3-5 Brainwriting
c. Fare
d. 180SearchAssistant

4. A _________ is the price one pays as remuneration for services, especially the honorarium paid to a doctor, lawyer, consultant, or other member of a learned profession. _________s usually allow for overhead, wages, costs, and markup.

Traditionally, professionals in Great Britain received a _________ in contradistinction to a payment, salary, or wage, and would often use guineas rather than pounds as units of account.

a. Transfer pricing
b. Price war
c. Price shading
d. Fee

5. _________ is a fee paid on borrowed assets. It is the price paid for the use of borrowed money , or, money earned by deposited funds . Assets that are sometimes lent with _________ include money, shares, consumer goods through hire purchase, major assets such as aircraft, and even entire factories in finance lease arrangements.

a. AMAX
b. ACNielsen
c. ADTECH
d. Interest

6. _________ in economics and business is the result of an exchange and from that trade we assign a numerical monetary value to a good, service or asset. If I trade 4 apples for an orange, the _________ of an orange is 4 - apples. Inversely, the _________ of an apple is 1/4 oranges.

a. Pricing
b. Contribution margin-based pricing
c. Discounts and allowances
d. Price

7. _________ is a rivalry between individuals, groups, nations for territory, a niche, or allocation of resources. It arises whenever two or more parties strive for a goal which cannot be shared. _________ occurs naturally between living organisms which co-exist in the same environment.

a. Competition
b. Price competition
c. Price fixing
d. Non-price competition

8. Non-_________ is a marketing strategy 'in which one firm tries to distinguish its product or service from competing products on the basis of attributes like design and workmanship' (McConnell-Brue, 2002, p. 437-438.) The firm can also distinguish its product offering through quality of service, extensive distribution, customer focus, or any other sustainable competitive advantage other than price.

a. Direct competition
b. Non-price competition
c. Price fixing
d. Price competition

9. _________ is a marketing strategy 'in which one firm tries to distinguish its product or service from competing products on the basis of attributes like design and workmanship' (McConnell-Brue, 2002, p. 437-438.) The firm can also distinguish its product offering through quality of service, extensive distribution, customer focus, or any other sustainable competitive advantage other than price.

a. Price competition
b. Price fixing
c. Direct competition
d. Non-price competition

10. In economics, _________ is the desire to own something and the ability to pay for it. The term _________ signifies the ability or the willingness to buy a particular commodity at a given point of time .

.

a. Market dominance
b. Discretionary spending
c. Demand
d. Market system

11. In economics, the _________ can be defined as the graph depicting the relationship between the price of a certain commodity, and the amount of it that consumers are willing and able to purchase at that given price. It is a graphic representation of a demand schedule The _________ for all consumers together follows from the _________ of every individual consumer: the individual demands at each price are added together.

_________s are used to estimate behaviors in competitive markets, and are often combined with supply curves to estimate the equilibrium price (the price at which sellers together are willing to sell the same amount as buyers together are willing to buy, also known as market clearing price) and the equilibrium quantity (the amount of that good or service that will be produced and bought without surplus/excess supply or shortage/excess demand) of that market.

a. 6-3-5 Brainwriting
b. 180SearchAssistant
c. Power III
d. Demand curve

12. _________ is defined as the measure of responsiveness in the quantity demanded for a commodity as a result of change in price of the same commodity. It is a measure of how consumers react to a change in price. In other words, it is percentage change in quantity demanded as per the percentage change in price of the same commodity.

a. 6-3-5 Brainwriting
b. 180SearchAssistant
c. Power III
d. Price elasticity of demand

13. In economics, _________ is the ratio of the percent change in one variable to the percent change in another variable. It is a tool for measuring the responsiveness of a function to changes in parameters in a relative way. Commonly analyzed are _________ of substitution, price and wealth.

a. ACNielsen
b. Elasticity
c. Opinion leadership
d. Intellectual property

14. Price _________ is defined as the measure of responsiveness in the quantity demanded for a commodity as a result of change in price of the same commodity. It is a measure of how consumers react to a change in price. In other words, it is percentage change in quantity demanded as per the percentage change in price of the same commodity.

a. ADTECH
b. AMAX
c. ACNielsen
d. Elasticity of Demand

15. In mathematics, an _________, or central tendency of a data set refers to a measure of the 'middle' or 'expected' value of the data set. There are many different descriptive statistics that can be chosen as a measurement of the central tendency of the data items.

An _________ is a single value that is meant to typify a list of values.

a. ACNielsen
b. ADTECH
c. AMAX
d. Average

16. _________ is an economics term used to describe the total fixed costs (TFC) divided by the quantity (Q) of units produced.

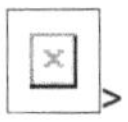

_________ is a per-unit measure of fixed costs. As the total number of goods produced increases, the _________ decreases because the same amount of fixed costs are being spread over a larger number of units.

a. ADTECH
b. Average fixed cost
c. Average variable cost
d. ACNielsen

17. In economics, _________ is equal to total cost divided by the number of goods produced (the output quantity, Q.) It is also equal to the sum of average variable costs (total variable costs divided by Q) plus average fixed costs (total fixed costs divided by Q.) _________s may be dependent on the time period considered (increasing production may be expensive or impossible in the short term, for example.)

a. ACNielsen
b. Average variable cost
c. ADTECH
d. Average cost

18. _________ is an economics term to describe a firms variable costs (labor, electricity, etc.) divided by the quantity (Q) of total units of output.

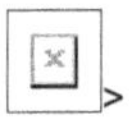

Where:

- TVC = Total Variable Cost
- _________ = Average variable cost
- Q = Quantity of Units Produced

_________ plus average fixed cost equals average total cost:

_________ + AFC = ATC.

.

a. ADTECH
b. Average fixed cost
c. ACNielsen
d. Average variable cost

19. In economics, business, retail, and accounting, a _________ is the value of money that has been used up to produce something, and hence is not available for use anymore. In economics, a _________ is an alternative that is given up as a result of a decision. In business, the _________ may be one of acquisition, in which case the amount of money expended to acquire it is counted as _________.

a. Fixed costs
b. Transaction cost
c. Variable cost
d. Cost

20. In economics, _________ are business expenses that are not dependent on the activities of the business They tend to be time-related, such as salaries or rents being paid per month. This is in contrast to variable costs, which are volume-related (and are paid per quantity.)

In management accounting, _________ are defined as expenses that do not change in proportion to the activity of a business, within the relevant period or scale of production.

a. Transaction cost
b. Marginal cost
c. Fixed costs
d. Variable cost

21. _________ is the use of marginal concepts within economics. (Marginal concepts are associated with a specific change in the quantity used of a good or of a service, as opposed to some notion of the over-all significance of that class of good or service, or of some total quantity thereof.) The central concept of _________ proper is that of marginal utility, but marginalists following the lead of Alfred Marshall were further heavily dependent upon the concept of marginal physical productivity in their explanation of cost; and the neoclassical tradition that emerged from British _________ generally abandoned the concept of utility and gave marginal rates of substitution a more fundamental rôle in analysis.

a. 180SearchAssistant
b. Power III
c. 6-3-5 Brainwriting
d. Marginalism

22. In economics and finance, _________ is the change in total cost that arises when the quantity produced changes by one unit. It is the cost of producing one more unit of a good. Mathematically, the _________ function is expressed as the first derivative of the total cost (TC) function with respect to quantity (Q.)

a. Transaction cost
b. Variable cost
c. Fixed costs
d. Marginal cost

23. In economics, and cost accounting, _________ describes the total economic cost of production and is made up of variable costs, which vary according to the quantity of a good produced and include inputs such as labor and raw materials, plus fixed costs, which are independent of the quantity of a good produced and include inputs (capital) that cannot be varied in the short term, such as buildings and machinery. _________ in economics includes the total opportunity cost of each factor of production in addition to fixed and variable costs.

The rate at which _________ changes as the amount produced changes is called marginal cost.

a. Hoarding
b. Product proliferation
c. Household production function
d. Total cost

24. _________s are used in open sentences. For instance, in the formula x + 1 = 5, x is a _________ which represents an 'unknown' number. _________s are often represented by letters of the Roman alphabet, or those of other alphabets, such as Greek, and use other special symbols.

a. Book of business
b. Variable
c. Quantitative
d. Personalization

25. _________s are expenses that change in proportion to the activity of a business. In other words, _________ is the sum of marginal costs. It can also be considered normal costs.

a. Transaction cost
b. Fixed costs
c. Marginal cost
d. Variable cost

26. The break-even point for a product is the point where total revenue received equals the total costs associated with the sale of the product (TR=TC.) A break-even point is typically calculated in order for businesses to determine if it would be profitable to sell a proposed product, as opposed to attempting to modify an existing product instead so it can be made lucrative. _________ can also be used to analyse the potential profitability of an expenditure in a sales-based business.

In _________, margin of safety is how much output or sales level can fall before a business reaches its break-even point (BEP).

a. Pay Per Sale
b. Contribution margin-based pricing
c. Price skimming
d. Break even analysis

27. In microeconomics, _________ is the extra revenue that an additional unit of product will bring. It is the additional income from selling one more unit of a good; sometimes equal to price. It can also be described as the change in total revenue/change in number of units sold.

a. Product proliferation
b. Marginal revenue
c. Hoarding
d. Total cost

28. _________ is defined by the American _________ Association as the activity, set of institutions, and processes for creating, communicating, delivering, and exchanging offerings that have value for customers, clients, partners, and society at large. The term developed from the original meaning which referred literally to going to market, as in shopping, or going to a market to sell goods or services.

_________ practice tends to be seen as a creative industry, which includes advertising, distribution and selling.

a. Product naming
b. Marketing myopia
c. Customer acquisition management
d. Marketing

29. The _________ is generally accepted as the use and specification of the four p's describing the strategic position of a product in the marketplace. One version of the origins of the _________ starts in 1948 when James Culliton said that a marketing decision should be a result of something similar to a recipe. This version continued in 1953 when Neil Borden, in his American Marketing Association presidential address, took the recipe idea one step further and coined the term 'Marketing-Mix'.

a. Power III
b. 6-3-5 Brainwriting
c. 180SearchAssistant
d. Marketing mix

30. A _________ is a collection of symbols, experiences and associations connected with a product, a service, a person or any other artifact or entity.

_________s have become increasingly important components of culture and the economy, now being described as 'cultural accessories and personal philosophies'.

Some people distinguish the psychological aspect of a _________ from the experiential aspect.

a. Brandable software
b. Store brand
c. Brand equity
d. Brand

31. _________ involves disseminating information about a product, product line, brand, or company. It is one of the four key aspects of the marketing mix. (The other three elements are product marketing, pricing, and distribution). P>_________ is generally sub-divided into two parts:

- Above the line _________: Promotion in the media (e.g. TV, radio, newspapers, Internet and Mobile Phones) in which the advertiser pays an advertising agency to place the ad
- Below the line _________: All other _________. Much of this is intended to be subtle enough for the consumer to be unaware that _________ is taking place. E.g. sponsorship, product placement, endorsements, sales _________, merchandising, direct mail, personal selling, public relations, trade shows

a. Davie Brown Index
b. Promotion
c. Cashmere Agency
d. Bottling lines

32. _________ is a broad label that refers to any individuals or households that use goods and services generated within the economy. The concept of a _________ is used in different contexts, so that the usage and significance of the term may vary.

A _________ is a person who uses any product or service.

a. Consumer
b. 180SearchAssistant
c. Power III
d. 6-3-5 Brainwriting

33. The _________ is an independent agency of the United States government, established in 1914 by the _________ Act. Its principal mission is the promotion of 'consumer protection' and the elimination and prevention of what regulators perceive to be harmfully 'anti-competitive' business practices, such as coercive monopoly.

The _________ Act was one of President Wilson's major acts against trusts.

a. 6-3-5 Brainwriting
b. Power III
c. 180SearchAssistant
d. Federal Trade Commission

34. The _________ of 1914 (15 U.S.C Â§Â§ 41-58, as amended) established the Federal Trade Commission (FTC), a bipartisan body of five members appointed by the President of the United States for seven year terms. This Commission was authorized to issue Cease and Desist orders to large corporations to curb unfair trade practices. This Act also gave more flexibility to the US congress for judicial matters.
a. Product liability
b. Gripe site
c. Comparative negligence
d. Federal Trade Commission Act

35. _________ refers to 'controlling human or societal behaviour by rules or restrictions.' _________ can take many forms: legal restrictions promulgated by a government authority, self-_________, social _________, co-_________ and market _________. One can consider _________ as actions of conduct imposing sanctions (such as a fine.) This action of administrative law, or implementing regulatory law, may be contrasted with statutory or case law.
a. CAN-SPAM
b. Rule of four
c. Regulation
d. Non-conventional trademark

36. The _________ requires the Federal government to investigate and pursue trusts, companies and organizations suspected of violating the Act. It was the first United States Federal statute to limit cartels and monopolies, and today still forms the basis for most antitrust litigation by the federal government.
a. Power III
b. 6-3-5 Brainwriting
c. 180SearchAssistant
d. Sherman Antitrust Act

37. The _________ of 1938 is a United States federal law that amended the Federal Trade Commission Act to add the clause 'unfair or deceptive acts or practices in commerce are hereby declared unlawful' to the Section 5 prohibition of unfair methods of competition, in order to protect consumers as well as competition.

1938 amendment to the federal trade commission act that authorized the FTC to restrict unfair or deceptive acts; also called the advertising act. Until this amendment was passed, the FTC could only restrict practices that were unfair to competitors.

a. Nutrition Labeling and Education Act
b. Patent
c. Sarbanes-Oxley Act of 2002
d. Wheeler-Lea Act

38. Regulation refers to 'controlling human or societal behaviour by rules or restrictions.' Regulation can take many forms: legal restrictions promulgated by a government authority, self-regulation, social regulation (e.g. norms), co-regulation and market regulation. One can consider regulation as actions of conduct imposing sanctions (such as a fine.) This action of administrative law, or implementing _________ law, may be contrasted with statutory or case law.

a. Right to Financial Privacy Act
b. Robinson-Patman Act
c. Privacy law
d. Regulatory

39. _________ exists when sales of identical goods or services are transacted at different prices from the same provider. In a theoretical market with perfect information, no transaction costs or prohibition on secondary exchange (or re-selling) to prevent arbitrage, _________ can only be a feature of monopoly and oligopoly markets, where market power can be exercised. Otherwise, the moment the seller tries to sell the same good at different prices, the buyer at the lower price can arbitrage by selling to the consumer buying at the higher price but with a tiny discount.

a. Price discrimination
b. Resale price maintenance
c. Penetration pricing
d. Price

40. The _________ of 1936 (or Anti-Price Discrimination Act, 15 U.S.C. Â§ 13) is a United States federal law that prohibits what were considered, at the time of passage, to be anticompetitive practices by producers, specifically price discrimination. It grew out of practices in which chain stores were allowed to purchase goods at lower prices than other retailers.

a. Registered trademark symbol
b. Fair Debt Collection Practices Act
c. Trademark infringement
d. Robinson-Patman Act

41. In business, a _________ is a product or a business unit that generates unusually high profit margins: so high that it is responsible for a large amount of a company's operating profit. This profit far exceeds the amount necessary to maintain the _________ business, and the excess is used by the business for other purposes.

A firm is said to be acting as a _________ when its earnings per share (EPS) is equal to its dividends per share (DPS), or in other words, when a firm pays out 100% of its free cash flow (FCF) to its shareholders as dividends at the end of each accounting term.

a. Goal setting
b. Cash cow
c. Crisis management
d. Corporate transparency

42. _________ is an economics term used to describe the system of firms setting prices of their goods the same to all buyers regardless of the sellers location, even if their transportation costs to the locations are different.

This means that if the destinations are far apart and have considerably different costs of transportation, each will still be charged the same price.

Although some consider this a form of collusion between the selling firms (it lowers the ability of buying firms to gain a competitive advantage by location or private transportation), it is common practice in the steel and automotive industries.

a. Price shading
b. Price war
c. Price markdown
d. Base point pricing

43. _________ is the study of the Earth and its lands, features, inhabitants, and phenomena. A literal translation would be 'to describe or write about the Earth'. The first person to use the word '_________' was Eratosthenes .

a. 180SearchAssistant
b. Power III
c. Geography
d. 6-3-5 Brainwriting

44. _________ is a technique used in propaganda and advertising. Also known as association, this is a technique of projecting positive or negative qualities (praise or blame) of a person, entity, object, or value (an individual, group, organization, nation, patriotism, etc.) to another in order to make the second more acceptable or to discredit it.

a. Micro ads
b. Sexism,
c. Supplier
d. Transfer

45. _________ refers to the pricing of contributions (assets, tangible and intangible, services, and funds) transferred within an organization. For example, goods from the production division may be sold to the marketing division, or goods from a parent company may be sold to a foreign subsidiary. Since the prices are set within an organization (i.e. controlled), the typical market mechanisms that establish prices for such transactions between third parties may not apply.

a. Fee
b. Transfer pricing
c. Price skimming
d. Discounts and allowances

1. _________ in economics and business is the result of an exchange and from that trade we assign a numerical monetary value to a good, service or asset. If I trade 4 apples for an orange, the _________ of an orange is 4 - apples. Inversely, the _________ of an apple is 1/4 oranges.

a. Price
b. Discounts and allowances
c. Pricing
d. Contribution margin-based pricing

2. _________ is one of the four Ps of the marketing mix. The other three aspects are product, promotion, and place. It is also a key variable in microeconomic price allocation theory.

a. Price
b. Competitor indexing
c. Relationship based pricing
d. Pricing

3. _________ or goals give direction to the whole pricing process. Determining what your objectives are is the first step in pricing. When deciding on _________ you must consider: 1) the overall financial, marketing, and strategic objectives of the company; 2) the objectives of your product or brand; 3) consumer price elasticity and price points; and 4) the resources you have available.

a. Transfer pricing
b. Pricing objectives
c. Discounts and allowances
d. Competitor indexing

4. _________, in strategic management and marketing, is the percentage or proportion of the total available market or market segment that is being serviced by a company. It can be expressed as a company's sales revenue (from that market) divided by the total sales revenue available in that market. It can also be expressed as a company's unit sales volume (in a market) divided by the total volume of units sold in that market.

a. Market share
b. Customer relationship management
c. Cyberdoc
d. Demand generation

5. The break-even point for a product is the point where total revenue received equals the total costs associated with the sale of the product (TR=TC.) A break-even point is typically calculated in order for businesses to determine if it would be profitable to sell a proposed product, as opposed to attempting to modify an existing product instead so it can be made lucrative. _________ can also be used to analyse the potential profitability of an expenditure in a sales-based business.

In _________, margin of safety is how much output or sales level can fall before a business reaches its break-even point (BEP).

a. Contribution margin-based pricing
b. Pay Per Sale
c. Break even analysis
d. Price skimming

6. _________ is systematic determination of merit, worth, and significance of something or someone using criteria against a set of standards. _________ often is used to characterize and appraise subjects of interest in a wide range of human enterprises, including the arts, criminal justice, foundations and non-profit organizations, government, health care, and other human services.

Depending on the topic of interest, there are professional groups which look to the quality and rigor of the _________ process.

a. AMAX
b. ADTECH
c. ACNielsen
d. Evaluation

7. _________ is a business term meaning the market segment to which a particular good or service is marketed. It is mainly defined by age, gender, geography, socio-economic grouping, technographic, or any other combination of demographics. It is generally studied and mapped by an organization through lists and reports containing demographic information that may have an effect on the marketing of key products or services.

a. Category Development Index
b. Brando
c. Distribution
d. Market specialization

8. _________ is a form of communication that typically attempts to persuade potential customers to purchase or to consume more of a particular brand of product or service. 'While now central to the contemporary global economy and the reproduction of global production networks, it is only quite recently that _________ has been more than a marginal influence on patterns of sales and production. The formation of modern _________ was intimately bound up with the emergence of new forms of monopoly capitalism around the end of the 19th and beginning of the 20th century as one element in corporate strategies to create, organize and where possible control markets, especially for mass produced consumer goods.

a. ACNielsen
b. AMAX
c. ADTECH
d. Advertising

9. _________ is a pricing method used by companies. It is used primarily because it is easy to calculate and requires little information. There are several varieties, but the common thread in all of them is that one first calculates the cost of the product, then includes an additional amount to represent profit.

a. Break even analysis
b. Loss leader
c. Cost-plus pricing
d. Relationship based pricing

10. The Oxford University Press defines _________ as 'marketing on a worldwide scale reconciling or taking commercial advantage of global operational differences, similarities and opportunities in order to meet global objectives.' Oxford University Press' Glossary of Marketing Terms.

Here are three reasons for the shift from domestic to _________ as given by the authors of the textbook, _________ Management--3rd Edition by Masaaki Kotabe and Kristiaan Helsen, 2004.

One of the product categories in which global competition has been easy to track is in U.S. automotive sales.

a. Diversity marketing
b. Digital marketing
c. Global marketing
d. Guerrilla Marketing

11. _________ is defined by the American _________ Association as the activity, set of institutions, and processes for creating, communicating, delivering, and exchanging offerings that have value for customers, clients, partners, and society at large. The term developed from the original meaning which referred literally to going to market, as in shopping, or going to a market to sell goods or services.

_________ practice tends to be seen as a creative industry, which includes advertising, distribution and selling.

a. Customer acquisition management
b. Marketing myopia
c. Product naming
d. Marketing

12. _________, also referred to as i-marketing, web marketing, online marketing is the marketing of products or services over the Internet.

The Internet has brought many unique benefits to marketing, one of which being lower costs for the distribution of information and media to a global audience. The interactive nature of _________, both in terms of providing instant response and eliciting responses, is a unique quality of the medium.

a. AMAX
b. ADTECH
c. Internet marketing
d. ACNielsen

13. _________ is the pricing technique of setting a relatively low initial entry price, often lower than the eventual market price, to attract new customers. The strategy works on the expectation that customers will switch to the new brand because of the lower price. _________ is most commonly associated with a marketing objective of increasing market share or sales volume, rather than to make profit in the short term.

a. Fee
b. Competitor indexing
c. Price war
d. Penetration pricing

14. _________ is a pricing strategy in which a marketer sets a relatively high price for a product or service at first, then lowers the price over time. It is a temporal version of price discrimination/yield management. It allows the firm to recover its sunk costs quickly before competition steps in and lowers the market price.

a. Discounts and allowances
b. Relationship based pricing
c. Price markdown
d. Price skimming

15. In retail sales, a _________ is a form of fraud in which the party putting forth the fraud lures in customers by advertising a product or service at an unprofitably low price, then reveals to potential customers that the advertised good is not available but that a substitute is.

The goal of the bait-and-switch is to convince some buyers to purchase the substitute good as a means of avoiding disappointment over not getting the bait, or as a way to recover sunk costs expended to try to obtain the bait. It suggests that the seller will not show the original product or product advertised but instead will demonstrate a more expensive product.

a. Roll-in
b. Bait and switch
c. Promotional products
d. Transpromotional

16. _________ is the practice of keeping the price of a product or service artificially high in order to encourage favorable perceptions among buyers, based solely on the price. The practice is intended to exploit the (not necessarily justifiable) tendency for buyers to assume that expensive items enjoy an exceptional reputation or represent exceptional quality and distinction.

The use of _________ as either a marketing strategy or a competitive practice depends on certain factors that influence its profitability and sustainability.

a. Price maintenance
b. Target costing
c. Price war
d. Premium pricing

17. _________ or price ending is a marketing practice based on the theory that certain prices have a psychological impact. The retail prices are often expressed as 'odd prices': a little less than a round number, e.g. $19.99 or Â£6.95 (but not necessarily mathematically odd, it could also be 2.98.) The theory is this drives demand greater than would be expected if consumers were perfectly rational.

a. Supplier diversity
b. First-mover advantage
c. Chain stores
d. Psychological pricing

18. _________ is a marketing strategy that involves offering several products for sale as one combined product. This strategy is very common in the software business (for example: bundle a word processor, a spreadsheet, and a database into a single office suite), in the cable television industry (for example, basic cable in the United States generally offers many channels at one price), and in the fast food industry in which multiple items are combined into a complete meal. A bundle of products is sometimes referred to as a package deal or a compilation or an anthology.

a. Psychographic
b. Primary research
c. Product bundling
d. Technology acceptance model

19. _________ occurs when cartels are illegal or overt collusion is absent. Put another way, two firms agree to play a certain strategy without explicitly saying so. This is also known as price leadership, as firms may stay within the law but still tacitly collude by monitoring each other's prices and keeping them the same. Usually, this occurs when a firm emerges to set the general industry price and other firms follow suit. Oligopolists usually try not to engage in price cutting, excessive advertising or other forms of competition.

a. Tacit collusion
b. Shop fitting
c. Chief privacy officer
d. Teaser rate

1. _________ is defined by the American _________ Association as the activity, set of institutions, and processes for creating, communicating, delivering, and exchanging offerings that have value for customers, clients, partners, and society at large. The term developed from the original meaning which referred literally to going to market, as in shopping, or going to a market to sell goods or services.

_________ practice tends to be seen as a creative industry, which includes advertising, distribution and selling.

a. Marketing myopia
b. Customer acquisition management
c. Product naming
d. Marketing

2. A _________ is a process that can allow an organization to concentrate its limited resources on the greatest opportunities to increase sales and achieve a sustainable competitive advantage. A _________ should be centered around the key concept that customer satisfaction is the main goal.

A _________ is most effective when it is an integral component of corporate strategy, defining how the organization will successfully engage customers, prospects, and competitors in the market arena.

a. Cyberdoc
b. Societal marketing
c. Psychographic
d. Marketing strategy

3. _________ is the realization of an application idea, model, design, specification, standard, algorithm an _________ is a realization of a technical specification or algorithm as a program, software component, or other computer system. Many _________s may exist for a given specification or standard.

a. ADTECH
b. Implementation
c. AMAX
d. ACNielsen

4. A _________ is a plan of action designed to achieve a particular goal.

_________ is different from tactics. In military terms, tactics is concerned with the conduct of an engagement while _________ is concerned with how different engagements are linked.

a. Power III
b. 6-3-5 Brainwriting
c. 180SearchAssistant
d. Strategy

5. In economics, an externality or spillover of an economic transaction is an impact on a party that is not directly involved in the transaction. In such a case, prices do not reflect the full costs or benefits in production or consumption of a product or service. A positive impact is called an _________ benefit, while a negative impact is called an _________ cost.

a. ACNielsen
b. ADTECH
c. External
d. AMAX

6. _________ is a technical term used in management science popularized by Joseph M. Juran

He defined an internal and external customers as anyone affected by the product or by the process used to produce the product, in the context of quality management. _________s may play the role as supplier, processer, and customer in the sequence of product development.

He claimed that the organization must understand and identify both internal and external customers and their needs.

a. ACNielsen
b. AMAX
c. ADTECH
d. Internal customer

7. _________ is an ongoing process that occurs strictly within a company or organization whereby the functional process aligns, motivates and empowers employees at all management levels to consistently deliver a satisfying customer experience. According to Burkitt and Zealley, 'the challenge for _________ is not only to get the right messages across, but to embed them in such a way that they both change and reinforce employee behaviour'.

a. ADTECH
b. AMAX
c. Internal marketing
d. ACNielsen

8. _________ involves disseminating information about a product, product line, brand, or company. It is one of the four key aspects of the marketing mix. (The other three elements are product marketing, pricing, and distribution). P>_________ is generally sub-divided into two parts:

- Above the line _________: Promotion in the media (e.g. TV, radio, newspapers, Internet and Mobile Phones) in which the advertiser pays an advertising agency to place the ad
- Below the line _________: All other _________. Much of this is intended to be subtle enough for the consumer to be unaware that _________ is taking place. E.g. sponsorship, product placement, endorsements, sales _________, merchandising, direct mail, personal selling, public relations, trade shows

a. Davie Brown Index
b. Promotion
c. Cashmere Agency
d. Bottling lines

9. _________ in economics and business is the result of an exchange and from that trade we assign a numerical monetary value to a good, service or asset. If I trade 4 apples for an orange, the _________ of an orange is 4 - apples. Inversely, the _________ of an apple is 1/4 oranges.

a. Price
b. Discounts and allowances
c. Contribution margin-based pricing
d. Pricing

10. _________ is a contract between two parties, one being the employer and the other being the employee. An employee may be defined as: 'A person in the service of another under any contract of hire, express or implied, oral or written, where the employer has the power or right to control and direct the employee in the material details of how the work is to be performed.' Black's Law Dictionary page 471 (5th ed. 1979.)

a. ACNielsen
b. Employment
c. ADTECH
d. AMAX

11. _________ is an advertisement in which a particular product specifically mentions a competitor by name for the express purpose of showing why the competitor is inferior to the product naming it.

This should not be confused with parody advertisements, where a fictional product is being advertised for the purpose of poking fun at the particular advertisement, nor should it be confused with the use of a coined brand name for the purpose of comparing the product without actually naming an actual competitor. ('Wikipedia tastes better and is less filling than the Encyclopedia Galactica.')

In the 1980s, during what has been referred to as the cola wars, soft-drink manufacturer Pepsi ran a series of advertisements where people, caught on hidden camera, in a blind taste test, chose Pepsi over rival Coca-Cola.

a. GL-70
b. Heavy-up
c. Cost per conversion
d. Comparative advertising

12. _________ is a business management strategy aimed at embedding awareness of quality in all organizational processes. _________ has been widely used in manufacturing, education, call centers, government, and service industries, as well as NASA space and science programs.

When used together as a phrase, the three words in this expression have the following meanings:

- Total: Involving the entire organization, supply chain, and/or product life cycle
- Quality: With its usual definitions, with all its complexities
- Management: The system of managing with steps like Plan, Organize, Control, Lead, Staff, provisioning and organizing.

As defined by the International Organization for Standardization (ISO):

> '_________ is a management approach for an organization, centered on quality, based on the participation of all its members and aiming at long-term success through customer satisfaction, and benefits to all members of the organization and to society.' ISO 8402:1994

One major aim is to reduce variation from every process so that greater consistency of effort is obtained. (Royse, D., Thyer, B., Padgett D., ' Logan T., 2006)

In Japan, _________ comprises four process steps, namely:

1. Kaizen - Focuses on 'Continuous Process Improvement', to make processes visible, repeatable and measurable.
2. Atarimae Hinshitsu - The idea that 'things will work as they are supposed to' .
3. Kansei - Examining the way the user applies the product leads to improvement in the product itself.
4. Miryokuteki Hinshitsu - The idea that 'things should have an aesthetic quality' (for example, a pen will write in a way that is pleasing to the writer.)

_________ requires that the company maintain this quality standard in all aspects of its business. This requires ensuring that things are done right the first time and that defects and waste are eliminated from operations.

a. 6-3-5 Brainwriting
b. Total quality management
c. Power III
d. 180SearchAssistant

13. _________ is the process of comparing the cost, cycle time, productivity, or quality of a specific process or method to another that is widely considered to be an industry standard or best practice. The result is often a business case for making changes in order to make improvements. The term _________ was first used by cobblers to measure ones feet for shoes.

a. Business strategy
b. Strategic group
c. Switching cost
d. Benchmarking

14. Quality management can be considered to have three main components: quality control, quality assurance and _________. Quality management is focused not only on product quality, but also the means to achieve it. Quality management therefore uses quality assurance and control of processes as well as products to achieve more consistent quality.

a. 6-3-5 Brainwriting
b. Power III
c. 180SearchAssistant
d. Quality improvement

15. Human beings are also considered to be _________ because they have the ability to change raw materials into valuable _________. The term Human _________ can also be defined as the skills, energies, talents, abilities and knowledge that are used for the production of goods or the rendering of services. While taking into account human beings as _________, the following things have to be kept in mind:

- The size of the population
- The capabilities of the individuals in that population

Many _________ cannot be consumed in their original form. They have to be processed in order to change them into more usable commodities.

a. 6-3-5 Brainwriting
b. 180SearchAssistant
c. Power III
d. Resources

16. A _________ is a list of the general tasks and responsibilities of a position. Typically, it also includes to whom the position reports, specifications such as the qualifications needed by the person in the job, salary range for the position, etc. A _________ is usually developed by conducting a job analysis, which includes examining the tasks and sequences of tasks necessary to perform the job.

a. Power III
b. 180SearchAssistant
c. Job description
d. 6-3-5 Brainwriting

17. _________ is the practice of individuals including commercial businesses, governments and institutions, facilitating the sale of their products or services to other companies or organizations that in turn resell them, use them as components in products or services they offer _________ is also called business-to-_________ for short. (Note that while marketing to government entities shares some of the same dynamics of organizational marketing, B2G Marketing is meaningfully different.)

a. Law of disruption
b. Mass marketing
c. Disruptive technology
d. Business marketing

18. _________ , according to The American Marketing Association, is 'a planning process designed to assure that all brand contacts received by a customer or prospect for a product, service, or organization are relevant to that person and consistent over time.' (Marketing Power Dictionary)

_________ is a term used to describe a holistic approach to marketing. It aims to ensure consistency of message and the complementary use of media. The concept includes online and offline marketing channels.

a. ADTECH
b. AMAX
c. ACNielsen
d. Integrated marketing communications

19. _________ refers to messages and related media used to communicate with a market. Those who practice advertising, branding, direct marketing, graphic design, marketing, packaging, promotion, publicity, sponsorship, public relations, sales, sales promotion and online marketing are termed marketing communicators, _________ managers, or more briefly as marcom managers.

a. Merchandising
b. Merchandise
c. Sales promotion
d. Marketing communication

20. _________ is a term used by inventory specialists to describe a level of stock that is maintained below the cycle stock to buffer against stockouts. _________ exists to counter uncertainties in supply and demand. _________ is defined as extra units of inventory carried as protection against possible stockouts.

a. Price-weighted
b. Safety stock
c. Product support
d. Cross-docking

21. In economics, business, retail, and accounting, a _________ is the value of money that has been used up to produce something, and hence is not available for use anymore. In economics, a _________ is an alternative that is given up as a result of a decision. In business, the _________ may be one of acquisition, in which case the amount of money expended to acquire it is counted as _________.

a. Fixed costs
b. Variable cost
c. Cost
d. Transaction cost

22. In economics, _________ are business expenses that are not dependent on the activities of the business They tend to be time-related, such as salaries or rents being paid per month. This is in contrast to variable costs, which are volume-related (and are paid per quantity.)

In management accounting, _________ are defined as expenses that do not change in proportion to the activity of a business, within the relevant period or scale of production.

a. Marginal cost
b. Fixed costs
c. Transaction cost
d. Variable cost

23. _________s are used in open sentences. For instance, in the formula x + 1 = 5, x is a _________ which represents an 'unknown' number. _________s are often represented by letters of the Roman alphabet, or those of other alphabets, such as Greek, and use other special symbols.

a. Personalization
b. Quantitative
c. Book of business
d. Variable

24. _________s are expenses that change in proportion to the activity of a business. In other words, _________ is the sum of marginal costs. It can also be considered normal costs.

a. Fixed costs
b. Marginal cost
c. Variable cost
d. Transaction cost

25. The break-even point for a product is the point where total revenue received equals the total costs associated with the sale of the product (TR=TC.) A break-even point is typically calculated in order for businesses to determine if it would be profitable to sell a proposed product, as opposed to attempting to modify an existing product instead so it can be made lucrative. _________ can also be used to analyse the potential profitability of an expenditure in a sales-based business.

In _________, margin of safety is how much output or sales level can fall before a business reaches its break-even point (BEP).

a. Price skimming
b. Break even analysis
c. Contribution margin-based pricing
d. Pay Per Sale

26. The general definition of an _________ is an evaluation of a person, organization, system, process, project or product. _________s are performed to ascertain the validity and reliability of information; also to provide an assessment of a system's internal control. The goal of an _________ is to express an opinion on the person/organization/system (etc) in question, under evaluation based on work done on a test basis.

a. ADTECH
b. Audit
c. AMAX
d. ACNielsen

27. _________ is the provision of service to customers before, during and after a purchase.

According to Turban et al., '_________ is a series of activities designed to enhance the level of customer satisfaction - that is, the feeling that a product or service has met the customer expectation.'

Its importance varies by product, industry and customer.

a. Customer experience
b. COPC Inc.
c. Facing
d. Customer service

1. _________ is defined by the American _________ Association as the activity, set of institutions, and processes for creating, communicating, delivering, and exchanging offerings that have value for customers, clients, partners, and society at large. The term developed from the original meaning which referred literally to going to market, as in shopping, or going to a market to sell goods or services.

_________ practice tends to be seen as a creative industry, which includes advertising, distribution and selling.

a. Marketing
b. Marketing myopia
c. Customer acquisition management
d. Product naming

2. _________, commonly known as e-commerce or eCommerce, consists of the buying and selling of products or services over electronic systems such as the Internet and other computer networks. The amount of trade conducted electronically has grown extraordinarily with wide-spread Internet usage. A wide variety of commerce is conducted in this way, spurring and drawing on innovations in electronic funds transfer, supply chain management, Internet marketing, online transaction processing, electronic data interchange (EDI), inventory management systems, and automated data collection systems.

a. ADTECH
b. AMAX
c. ACNielsen
d. Electronic commerce

3. Electronic commerce, commonly known as _________ or eCommerce, consists of the buying and selling of products or services over electronic systems such as the Internet and other computer networks. The amount of trade conducted electronically has grown extraordinarily with wide-spread Internet usage. A wide variety of commerce is conducted in this way, spurring and drawing on innovations in electronic funds transfer, supply chain management, Internet marketing, online transaction processing, electronic data interchange (EDI), inventory management systems, and automated data collection systems.

a. AMAX
b. ACNielsen
c. E-commerce
d. ADTECH

4. In computing, a _________ is a type of Uniform Resource Identifier (URI) that specifies where an identified resource is available and the mechanism for retrieving it. In popular usage and in many technical documents and verbal discussions it is often incorrectly used as a synonym for URI. In popular language, a _________ is also referred to as a Web address.

a. Uniform Resource Locator
b. AMAX
c. ACNielsen
d. ADTECH

5. _________ is a business term meaning the market segment to which a particular good or service is marketed. It is mainly defined by age, gender, geography, socio-economic grouping, technographic, or any other combination of demographics. It is generally studied and mapped by an organization through lists and reports containing demographic information that may have an effect on the marketing of key products or services.

a. Category Development Index
b. Market specialization
c. Brando
d. Distribution

6. A _________ is a process that can allow an organization to concentrate its limited resources on the greatest opportunities to increase sales and achieve a sustainable competitive advantage. A _________ should be centered around the key concept that customer satisfaction is the main goal.

A _________ is most effective when it is an integral component of corporate strategy, defining how the organization will successfully engage customers, prospects, and competitors in the market arena.

a. Cyberdoc
b. Societal marketing
c. Psychographic
d. Marketing strategy

7. _________ is a term commonly used to describe commerce transactions between businesses like the one between a manufacturer and a wholesaler or a wholesaler and a retailer i.e both the buyer and the seller are business entity.This is unlike business-to-consumers (B2C) which involve a business entity and end consumer, or business-to-government (B2G) which involve a business entity and government.

The volume of B2B transactions is much higher than the volume of B2C transactions. The primary reason for this is that in a typical supply chain there will be many B2B transactions involving subcomponent or raw materials, and only one B2C transaction, specifically sale of the finished product to the end customer.

a. Disruptive technology
b. Business-to-business
c. Social marketing
d. Customer relationship management

8. _________ describes activities of businesses serving end consumers with products and/or services.

An example of a B2C transaction would be a person buying a pair of shoes from a retailer. The transactions that led to the shoes being available for purchase, that is the purchase of the leather, laces, rubber, etc.

a. Societal marketing
b. Business-to-consumer
c. Corporate capabilities package
d. Demand generation

9. _________ (or citizen-to-citizen) electronic commerce involves the electronically-facilitated transactions between consumers through some third party. A common example is the online auction, in which a consumer posts an item for sale and other consumers bid to purchase it; the third party generally charges a flat fee or commission. The sites are only intermediaries, just there to match consumers.

a. Consumer-to-consumer
b. Web banner
c. Business-to-government
d. Locator software

10. In marketing, _________ is the process of distinguishing the differences of a product or offering from others, to make it more attractive to a particular target market. This involves differentiating it from competitors' products as well as one's own product offerings.

Differentiation is a source of competitive advantage.

a. Packshot
b. Corporate image
c. Product differentiation
d. Marketing myopia

11. _________ is one of the four elements of marketing mix. An organization or set of organizations (go-betweens) involved in the process of making a product or service available for use or consumption by a consumer or business user.

The other three parts of the marketing mix are product, pricing, and promotion.

a. Better Living Through Chemistry
b. Comparison-Shopping agent
c. Distribution
d. Japan Advertising Photographers' Association

12. _________ is a form of communication that typically attempts to persuade potential customers to purchase or to consume more of a particular brand of product or service. 'While now central to the contemporary global economy and the reproduction of global production networks, it is only quite recently that _________ has been more than a marginal influence on patterns of sales and production. The formation of modern _________ was intimately bound up with the emergence of new forms of monopoly capitalism around the end of the 19th and beginning of the 20th century as one element in corporate strategies to create, organize and where possible control markets, especially for mass produced consumer goods.
a. ACNielsen
b. ADTECH
c. AMAX
d. Advertising

13. _________ involves disseminating information about a product, product line, brand, or company. It is one of the four key aspects of the marketing mix. (The other three elements are product marketing, pricing, and distribution). P>_________ is generally sub-divided into two parts:

- Above the line _________: Promotion in the media (e.g. TV, radio, newspapers, Internet and Mobile Phones) in which the advertiser pays an advertising agency to place the ad
- Below the line _________: All other _________. Much of this is intended to be subtle enough for the consumer to be unaware that _________ is taking place. E.g. sponsorship, product placement, endorsements, sales _________, merchandising, direct mail, personal selling, public relations, trade shows

a. Cashmere Agency
b. Bottling lines
c. Davie Brown Index
d. Promotion

14. _________ is the deliberate attempt to manage the public's perception of a subject. The subjects of _________ include people (for example, politicians and performing artists), goods and services, organizations of all kinds, and works of art or entertainment.

From a marketing perspective, _________ is one component of promotion.

a. Little value placed on potential benefits
b. Brando
c. Pearson's chi-square
d. Publicity

15. A _________ or banner ad is a form of advertising on the World Wide Web. This form of online advertising entails embedding an advertisement into a web page. It is intended to attract traffic to a website by linking to the website of the advertiser.
a. Spamvertising
b. Disintermediation
c. Consumer privacy
d. Web banner

16. _________ is a way of measuring the success of an online advertising campaign. A CTR is obtained by dividing the number of users who clicked on an ad on a web page by the number of times the ad was delivered (impressions.) For example, if a banner ad was delivered 100 times (impressions delivered) and one person clicked on it (clicks recorded), then the resulting CTR would be 1 percent.

a. Web analytics
b. JICIMS
c. Display advertising
d. Click-through rate

17. The Oxford University Press defines _________ as 'marketing on a worldwide scale reconciling or taking commercial advantage of global operational differences, similarities and opportunities in order to meet global objectives.' Oxford University Press' Glossary of Marketing Terms.

Here are three reasons for the shift from domestic to _________ as given by the authors of the textbook, _________ Management--3rd Edition by Masaaki Kotabe and Kristiaan Helsen, 2004.

One of the product categories in which global competition has been easy to track is in U.S. automotive sales.

a. Digital marketing
b. Guerrilla Marketing
c. Diversity marketing
d. Global marketing

18. _________, also referred to as i-marketing, web marketing, online marketing is the marketing of products or services over the Internet.

The Internet has brought many unique benefits to marketing, one of which being lower costs for the distribution of information and media to a global audience. The interactive nature of _________, both in terms of providing instant response and eliciting responses, is a unique quality of the medium.

a. AMAX
b. ACNielsen
c. ADTECH
d. Internet marketing

19. An _________ is an advertisement written in the form of an objective opinion editorial, and presented in a printed publication--usually designed to look like a legitimate and independent news story.

_________s differ from traditional advertisements in that they are designed to look like the articles that appear in the publication.

a. ACNielsen
b. ADTECH
c. Informative advertising
d. Advertorial

20. _________ are a form of online advertising on the World Wide Web intended to attract web traffic or capture email addresses. It works when certain web sites open a new web browser window to display advertisements. The pop-up window containing an advertisement is usually generated by JavaScript, but can be generated by other means as well.

a. Customer intelligence
b. Project Portfolio Management
c. Power III
d. Pop-up ads

21. _________ is one of the four aspects of promotional mix. (The other three parts of the promotional mix are advertising, personal selling, and publicity/public relations.) Media and non-media marketing communication are employed for a pre-determined, limited time to increase consumer demand, stimulate market demand or improve product availability.

a. Merchandise
b. New Media Strategies
c. Marketing communication
d. Sales promotion

22. The _________ is an American federal law (codified at 15 U.S.C. Â§ 1681 et seq.) that regulates the collection, dissemination, and use of consumer credit information.

a. 6-3-5 Brainwriting
b. Fair Credit Reporting Act
c. 180SearchAssistant
d. Power III

23. The _________ is a marketing term and refers to all of the forces outside of marketing that affect marketing management's ability to build and maintain successful relationships with target customers. The _________ consists of both the macroenvironment and the microenvironment.

The microenvironment refers to the forces that are close to the company and affect its ability to serve its customers.

a. Market environment
b. Psychographic
c. Business-to-consumer
d. Customer franchise

24. _________ in economics and business is the result of an exchange and from that trade we assign a numerical monetary value to a good, service or asset. If I trade 4 apples for an orange, the _________ of an orange is 4 - apples. Inversely, the _________ of an apple is 1/4 oranges.

a. Contribution margin-based pricing
b. Pricing
c. Discounts and allowances
d. Price

25. _________ is the ability of an individual or group to seclude themselves or information about themselves and thereby reveal themselves selectively. The boundaries and content of what is considered private differ among cultures and individuals, but share basic common themes. _________ is sometimes related to anonymity, the wish to remain unnoticed or unidentified in the public realm.

a. Privacy
b. Power III
c. 180SearchAssistant
d. 6-3-5 Brainwriting

26. The _________, is a United States Act that gives the customers of financial institutions the right to some level of privacy from government searches. Before the Act was passed, the United States government did not have to tell customers that they were accessing their records, and customers did not have the right to prevent such actions.

a. Wheeler-Lea Act
b. Real property
c. Copyright
d. Right to Financial Privacy Act

27. _________ is a branch of philosophy which seeks to address questions about morality, such as how a moral outcome can be achieved in a specific situation (applied _________), how moral values should be determined (normative _________), what moral values people actually abide by (descriptive _________), what the fundamental semantic, ontological, and epistemic nature of _________ or morality is (meta-_________), and how moral capacity or moral agency develops and what its nature is (moral psychology.)

Socrates was one of the first Greek philosophers to encourage both scholars and the common citizen to turn their attention from the outside world to the condition of man. In this view, Knowledge having a bearing on human life was placed highest, all other knowledge being secondary.

a. Ethics
b. AMAX
c. ADTECH
d. ACNielsen

28. _________ is one of the four Ps of the marketing mix. The other three aspects are product, promotion, and place. It is also a key variable in microeconomic price allocation theory.

a. Price
b. Competitor indexing
c. Pricing
d. Relationship based pricing

29. _________ refer to a collection of facts usually collected as the result of experience, observation or experiment or a set of premises. This may consist of numbers, words particularly as measurements or observations of a set of variables. _________ are often viewed as a lowest level of abstraction from which information and knowledge are derived.

a. Data
b. Sample size
c. Pearson product-moment correlation coefficient
d. Mean

1. _________ is a management idea which asserts that there is a technique, method, process, activity, incentive or reward that is more effective at delivering a particular outcome than any other technique, method, process, etc.

a. Thing

b. Best practice24

c. Undefined

d. Undefined

Chapter 1

1. c	2. b	3. d	4. c	5. d	6. c	7. d	8. d	9. c	10. d
11. d	12. c	13. a	14. a	15. d	16. d	17. c	18. a		

Chapter 2

1. d	2. a	3. d	4. d	5. d	6. d	7. d	8. d	9. c	10. a
11. b	12. d	13. b	14. d	15. d	16. b	17. a	18. d	19. c	20. b
21. d	22. d	23. d	24. b	25. c	26. d	27. a	28. b	29. b	30. b

Chapter 3

1. d	2. a	3. b	4. a	5. b	6. d	7. a	8. b	9. d	10. c
11. c	12. a	13. c	14. c	15. a	16. d	17. a	18. d	19. b	20. d
21. d	22. c	23. a	24. d	25. d	26. d	27. a	28. d	29. d	30. b
31. c	32. d	33. d	34. d	35. d	36. d	37. d	38. a	39. d	40. d
41. d	42. c	43. c	44. d	45. d	46. b	47. c	48. b	49. d	50. a
51. a	52. d	53. c							

Chapter 4

1. d	2. c	3. d	4. d	5. b	6. d	7. c	8. a	9. a	10. d
11. b	12. d								

Chapter 5

1. d	2. c	3. d	4. d	5. a	6. d	7. a	8. b	9. b	10. d
11. a	12. d	13. d	14. d	15. d	16. d	17. a	18. c	19. a	20. a
21. b	22. d	23. b	24. d	25. c	26. d	27. b	28. c		

Chapter 6

1. b	2. d	3. d	4. d	5. c	6. b	7. b	8. d	9. c	10. c
11. c	12. d	13. a	14. d	15. a	16. d	17. d	18. c	19. a	20. c
21. d	22. b	23. d	24. b	25. d	26. d	27. b	28. c	29. b	30. a

Chapter 7

1. b	2. d	3. b	4. a	5. d	6. d	7. d	8. b	9. d	10. c
11. c	12. a	13. a	14. b	15. d	16. a	17. c	18. b	19. a	20. c
21. d	22. c	23. b	24. c						

Chapter 8

1. a	2. d	3. b	4. c	5. a	6. a	7. b	8. d	9. d	10. d
11. d	12. c	13. a	14. c	15. d	16. d	17. c	18. c	19. d	20. d
21. d	22. d								

Chapter 9

1. d	2. b	3. d	4. b	5. d	6. c	7. d	8. c	9. d	10. c
11. b	12. d	13. d	14. d	15. a	16. b	17. d	18. b	19. d	20. d

Chapter 10

1. b	2. b	3. c	4. d	5. d	6. a	7. a	8. d	9. a	10. d
11. d									

Chapter 11

1. d	2. d	3. b	4. c	5. c	6. d	7. c	8. d	9. b	10. d
11. a	12. c	13. c	14. d	15. a	16. b	17. b	18. d	19. a	20. b

Chapter 12

1. c	2. d	3. d	4. d	5. d	6. d	7. d	8. a	9. c	10. b
11. d	12. a	13. b	14. d	15. a	16. d	17. c	18. d	19. a	20. c
21. b	22. d	23. d	24. a	25. b					

Chapter 13

1. c	2. d	3. c	4. c	5. d	6. d	7. d	8. a	9. d	10. b
11. d	12. b	13. b	14. d	15. b	16. a	17. d	18. d	19. a	20. a

Chapter 14

1. a	2. c	3. b	4. c	5. d	6. c	7. d	8. a	9. d	10. d
11. d									

Chapter 15

1. d	2. c	3. d	4. c	5. d	6. a	7. d	8. d	9. d	10. a
11. d	12. c	13. b	14. a	15. d	16. d	17. c	18. d	19. d	20. d
21. b	22. d	23. d	24. d						

Chapter 16

1. b	2. c	3. c	4. d	5. d	6. c	7. a	8. d	9. d	10. d
11. d	12. b	13. d	14. c	15. d	16. d	17. b	18. d	19. c	20. d

Chapter 17

1. a	2. d	3. b	4. a	5. b	6. d	7. d	8. c	9. d	10. c
11. d	12. d	13. d	14. d	15. b	16. d	17. d	18. d	19. c	20. a
21. d	22. d								

Chapter 18

1. d	2. d	3. d	4. d	5. b	6. a	7. b	8. c	9. b	10. b
11. d	12. d	13. d	14. d	15. b	16. d	17. a	18. d	19. c	20. b
21. d									

Chapter 19

1. d	2. d	3. d	4. d	5. d	6. b	7. d	8. b	9. b	10. b
11. b	12. d	13. d	14. b	15. d	16. d	17. d	18. b	19. d	20. d
21. d	22. d	23. c							

Chapter 20

1. d	2. a	3. c	4. d	5. d	6. d	7. a	8. d	9. d	10. c
11. d	12. d	13. b	14. d	15. d	16. b	17. d	18. d	19. d	20. c
21. d	22. d	23. d	24. b	25. d	26. d	27. b	28. d	29. d	30. d
31. b	32. a	33. d	34. d	35. c	36. d	37. d	38. d	39. a	40. d
41. b	42. d	43. c	44. d	45. b					

Chapter 21

1. a	2. d	3. b	4. a	5. c	6. d	7. d	8. d	9. c	10. c
11. d	12. c	13. d	14. d	15. b	16. d	17. d	18. c	19. a	

Chapter 22

1. d	2. d	3. b	4. d	5. c	6. d	7. c	8. b	9. a	10. b
11. d	12. b	13. d	14. d	15. d	16. c	17. d	18. d	19. d	20. b
21. c	22. b	23. d	24. c	25. b	26. b	27. d			

Chapter 23

1. a	2. d	3. c	4. a	5. b	6. d	7. b	8. b	9. a	10. c
11. c	12. d	13. d	14. d	15. d	16. d	17. d	18. d	19. d	20. d
21. d	22. b	23. a	24. d	25. a	26. d	27. a	28. c	29. a	

Chapter 24

1. b

www.ingramcontent.com/pod-product-compliance
Lightning Source LLC
Chambersburg PA
CBHW082045230426
43670CB00016B/2787
* 9 7 8 1 4 2 8 8 6 9 4 5 5 *